UNLEASH YOUR BEST SELF

DISCOVER THE MULTIPLIER EFFECTS TO YOUR SUCCESS

UNLEASH YOUR BEST SELF

DISCOVER THE MULTIPLIER EFFECTS TO YOUR SUCCESS

Joseph Iannicelli

ISBN 978-1-7776255-1-1 (paperback)
ISBN #978-1-7776255-2-8 (e-book)
ISBN #978-1-7776255-3-5 (hardcover)

Cover & Book Design by: Sandra Gauthier
Edited by: Maggie Morris (The Indie Editor), Sandra Gauthier
Additional Assistance: The Studio Press, Conker Press, Darlene Poier

To everyone that strives to be their best self...

Be the Multiplier Effect that makes you,
and all living things around you,
achieve the greatness that awaits.

ACKNOWLEDGMENTS

To my parents, Carolina and Vincenzo, for their unwavering love and support.

To my wife, Mary, and children, Carolyn, Vincent and Samuel, who inspire me to be my best every day.

To everyone and everything that has in some way been a Multiplier Effect in my life, you have all helped me write this book and I am grateful.

CONTENTS

INTRODUCTION

Once upon a time, I would have said that I did not win the Lucky Gene Lottery, but before I get to that, what even is that? Well . . .

The Past

I refer to this lottery as the lottery of genetic luck. You are a winner or loser depending on the socio-economic circumstances of your parents. If you win, you are born into wealth, privilege and opportunity. You know, royalty or the offspring of prominent, successful and financially fortunate individuals—lucky people like that.

When I was growing up, I soon realized that I was not a lucky winner and comparing myself to those who did win made me feel inferior, intimidated and not worthy of their company. I felt a definite lack of belonging.

The Present

Without realizing it, every single one of us is born into the wealth, privilege and opportunities the world has to offer, and we're all worthy of its abundance. Everything we need to be our best selves, 100 percent of the time, is readily available to us, BUT we just need to know where and how to look for it.

The Future

When we find what we need, we reach the zenith of our possibilities as human beings. For twenty-five years, I had the pleasure of working in the financial services industry and twenty of those were spent at the Standard Life Assurance Company of Canada. I refer to it simply as Standard Life. Throughout my career, I have been fortunate to meet and develop friendships with many financially successful people, most of whom were born into middle-class or more affluent families. They attended excellent schools, predominately private, and they obtained professional designations or postsecondary degrees. These people had successful careers that spanned decades, and postretirement, many became board members of prestigious companies or continued their corporate lives in some part-time manner.

Using a very broad definition, essentially, they've done the same thing always. They started in the corporate world, had success there and are now on boards, consulting, or advising in some way. Some spend time on hobbies, paying attention to things they were always interested in, but very few have begun something entirely new. I believed that this was a natural evolution and that my career and postretirement path would be consistent with this pattern. This mindset results in living within self-constructed boundaries of what you know and what you're comfortable with. Usually, we're comfortable with what we know and uncomfortable with what we don't. That is something I call living within barriers, from a perspective of experience, knowledge and intelligence. This is our comfort zone.

There is a fundamental flaw to living within our comfort zone. It severely limits our ability to expand the barriers beyond what we already know. When we realize that there is so much more to learn and that much of this exists beyond what we define as our comfort zone, life can be much more enriching. It will help you to live as a 100 percent human being—to live to your fullest capability—and your life will be remembered not as a novel but as a series of amazing short stories.

That is how I view my life—a series of short stories within what will hopefully be a very long book! Once a short story is concluded, I turn the page, and a new tale comes to life.

After retiring as CEO of Standard Life, I became an actor and producer in an industry that I had great interest in but knew nothing about. During that time, I was fortunate enough to produce a feature film that won multiple awards. Next, I trained as a yoga instructor, something I knew very little about but was attracted to for its history, influence on culture and the physical and mental benefits it was renowned for. It was only natural that I then became interested in the power of healing energy and started studying to become a Reiki Master. With each new challenge, I found excitement because the learning curve is so steep. What can be more exhilarating than diving into something completely new and learning as much as you can from it? Thus, each new adventure is a new short story, and it begins with an interest I know truly little about. These challenges and adventures are pathways to becoming my best and complete self as a human being.

As we go through each chapter of this book, let's consider what we can do to make ourselves, and each other, our ultimate selves.

As I pause to catch my breath, I look up and ask . . . Why? And what am I doing here?

I was conceived in Naples, Italy, the city best known as the birthplace of modern pizza, and for Sophia Loren, the Amalfi Coast and Mount Vesuvius, but I was not born there.

My father was one of sixteen children, and he walked to the beat of his own drum. While working in Italy, he always saved some money to visit family in New York, going back and forth often, until one day, at thirty-three years old, he felt it was time to settle down and get married. My parents had known each other since they were kids, as both families lived on the same street in Naples. My mom, the oldest of seven children, was one of the two main income earners in the household. Her father had passed away when she was just a teen, and at twenty-seven years old, when my story begins, it was considered unlikely that she'd marry. In fact, she had no intention of doing so, feeling responsible for her family. That did not deter my dad. He proposed anyway, and my grandmother, Nonna Assunta, gave Mom some wise words: "I love you and will miss you, but if you don't get married now, you'll never get married."

Dad had been sponsored to move to Canada by his sister, who already lived in Toronto, but when my parents found out they were pregnant, they knew that for their baby to be presented with more opportunities in life, that child must be born in Canada. This accelerated the time frame. My dad left immediately for Toronto and left Mom behind while he worked to earn enough money for her ticket. When the time finally arrived, my mother convinced her doctor to write a letter stating that she was seven months pregnant. In truth, she was eight. The trip to Canada took approximately one month, and it was not a good idea for pregnant women of eight months or more to be on the boat, in case they went into labor. That was my mom though. If she was determined to do something, there was no stopping her, even if that meant bending the rules to do it. She wanted me to be born in Canada, and so she did what was needed to make that happen.

Thanks to my mother's tenacity and the doctor's letter, she arrived in Halifax on September 16, 1961, took the train to Toronto, and I was born not long after on Oct 6, 1961.

I started life as the only son of Italian immigrants, whose parents did not exceed a third-grade education. I had a stable childhood that stood as a solid foundation on which I was able to create and reach my dreams. We lived in a predominantly Italian neighborhood in Downsview, Ontario, and my upbringing was in a typical lower-middle-class family. We didn't have access to a lot of money, but we wanted for nothing, and my parents gave me riches by giving me all the love and support I needed. It was an idyllic childhood.

The neighborhood kids and I would fish at the creek near the park, finding joy in nature and each other. Our bicycles were used for transportation, not exercise, and we walked to school regardless of the weather, but of course, we always came home for lunch to a delicious meal—Italians and food . . . it's a thing.

> *Don't think about what you don't have. Think about the greatest thing that you possess, the universe. It is yours, and no one can take it from you.*

We never thought about what we didn't have. That was never a way of thinking in our household. Instead, we thoroughly enjoyed what we did have. Nothing went to waste, and everything was reused and repurposed. We were recycling long before it was fashionable.

To this day, my family do their best to continue this lifestyle, and we try not to waste a thing, especially time. I carried that attitude and philosophy with me into my professional career. Time was money, and I never seemed to have enough of it; therefore, I needed to be mindful of how I spent it.

Growing up as an Italian, food was an essential part of our daily lives. Meals were always discussed at length, and I recall talking about what we were going to have for dinner while still having lunch. The strict instruction my father gave to my mother, who was the main grocery shopper, was to be careful with our money but never compromise on what we ate. That same rule applies in my home today.

My parents taught me to spend wisely and generously on what was important, while spending not much, if anything, on what wasn't. They never owned credit cards because they despised debt, and if we could make do or make it ourselves, we did. If we did have to purchase anything, it was always of the best quality that we could afford because it had to last. It never crossed our minds that maybe we were lacking in anything, but that's because we lacked nothing. We made do with what we had and did it with a grateful heart. It was fantastic.

Why Buy It When You Can Make It?

My parents did an incredible job of teaching me how to stretch every dollar as far as it could go, and sports equipment serves as a good example of this. Our baseball gloves in the summer doubled as road hockey goalie gloves in winter. We could only afford one hockey stick, so my mother's old straw broom made a great substitute for a goal stick, and our goalie blockers were made of heavy-duty cardboard. This was a simple design: cut out a rectangular piece of cardboard, make a couple of holes, weave old shoestrings through them, then tie it around the winter glove and voilà, a blocker. Even the ball was reused—a worn-out tennis ball that we'd ground down by rubbing it on the curb until only the rubber core remained.

Golf was another activity we played a lot but not at a real golf course. Instead, we dug holes on each side of the local park for an instant par 3. Did we have money to purchase golf clubs? You guessed correctly; we did not, but there was a company that manufactured golf clubs close to where we lived, and at night, when the factory was closed, we rode our bikes there and climbed into the garbage bins to see what we could find. Sometimes that would be faulty clubs, deemed unfit for sale, but they were good enough for us, and Dad would often weld the head to the shaft of the club if that was where the fault lay.

Hockey sticks had to last for at least two seasons as Dad wouldn't buy new ones every year, but Mom, who was working in a factory making fiberglass boats at the time, came up with an ingenious idea. If we purchased the least expensive stick on the market, basically a piece of kindling disguised as a hockey stick, she could take it to work and cover the blade in fiberglass. It was a brilliant idea, but when she brought it home, the stick was as solid as a rock, bottom-heavy and difficult to handle. Did it matter? No, and it did last for two years. We did eventually retire it with full honors, and it went on to a new life as a tomato stake in the vegetable garden.

As an only child with parents who worked shifts, I spent much of my indoor time alone. Television for kids was limited in those days, so I became a voracious reader, and although my favorites were stories about outer space and adventure, I'd read anything. One time, a fellow reader friend from school and I challenged each other to see who could read all of the books on a randomly selected bookshelf the fastest. We wrote down the names of all those books and got started. I can't recall exactly who won, but let's just assume it was me.

A lot of my time was spent alone daydreaming, visualizing myself as a character in whichever book I was reading—usually the lead. I thought about what it would be like to live in the world portrayed in the book, and that's something I still do to this day.

At school, I was the class clown, and I craved attention, so it was no surprise that I wanted to be an actor after high school. My plan was to enroll at Ryerson Polytechnic Institute (which has since been designated a university), in their Radio and Television Arts Program. All students were required to meet with the school counselor prior to finalizing their choices; Father Mark, who was ours, viewed my application and quickly discouraged me from applying. He said that it would be difficult to carve out a career in this field, especially in Toronto in the 1980s. Discouraged, I left his office and went home. Then I spoke to my dad about what I had in mind. It didn't go well. "Absolutely not! I did not come to this country so that you can be unemployed. You are going to university, and you will study business." So that was that. Economics at York University it was.

I definitely didn't feel like I won the Lucky Gene Lottery, as I needed to work hard for most things, but I developed what some would call street smarts, and that's something that is quite often more valuable than book smarts. A blend of practical experience and classroom experience is the best education one can obtain, in my opinion.

Talking about that reminds me of a conversation I once had with a tycoon in the business world for whom I have much admiration and respect. During that conversation, he told me that he admired me, not just for the role I held as President and CEO of Standard Life, but also for how I'd gotten there. He suggested that he admired me because, in his view, I had achieved success on my own. I was surprised and flattered. I thought about it for a minute. I didn't have a family inheritance or a family business to fall into my lap. My parents didn't help me get into university, nor did they help me get a job. I always worked hard. Yes, he's right! Later on in this book, I admit to the infinite number of ways that I have been helped by so many people, but at that moment, I thought, Wow, what a nice comment.

It was after that conversation that I realized I actually did win the Lucky Gene Lottery! But while I didn't have a clear understanding of what that meant, I figured it out, and it's quite simple—I have always had everything that I needed to succeed in life.

My parents are the reason I am who I am today. Their influence, drive and work ethic helped shape me, and I am convinced that I wouldn't be as blessed and fortunate had they not raised me in the environment they did, with the mindsets they had. It was the most stable foundation, and it became my responsibility to build whatever life I chose to create.

The reality is, the Lucky Gene Lottery is not a lottery at all. If we become our best self, we all win.

Why did I write this book?

My journey has led me to a place where my main purpose is to help people become the best they can be. Many of my clients, students and colleagues have encouraged me to pen my experiences so they can be shared with the world. I draw on my personal and professional experiences to guide you through a journey of self-discovery and self-mastery so you can unleash your maximum potential as a human being.

More and more people of all ages are looking at their personal and professional lives and wonder, "Is this it? Life is supposed to be easier than this." Despite a huge number of innovations designed to make lives easier and more stress free, everyone is experiencing more anxiety and stress than ever. Why? Social media, peer and parent pressure, increased competition, higher expectations, and too much information are all contributing factors. These are all external factors whose effects are exaggerated in the absence of self-awareness and self-confidence. As a result, they settle for "good enough" in most instances. This eventually leads to frustration and lack of sense of fulfilment, and they are now asking themselves, "Is this what I really want to do and be?", "Am I happy?", "Can I be more successful at work?", "Can I be more successful in life? "Am I living my fullest life?" *Unleash Your Best Self* will help you understand that you are where you are as a result of your life lived to date and that you can do so much more to become what you are ultimately supposed to be. This will lead to health, happiness and success.

CHAPTER 1

Who Are You?

You Don't Want These Hands

I love my dad more today than the day he passed away. April 6, 1988 was when he transitioned, and I'll never forget it because I was there at his bedside. I just sat and watched his breathing, wondering what happens when someone is close to the end of their life. Is there a clear guided path with a welcoming party ready to greet you? Is there a sense of ease, perhaps relief? I was angry and selfish because I still needed him. There was so much more to do and learn. How dare he leave me so soon? I still needed him and would be somewhat lost without him.

As he took his final breath, I reached down to close his eyes, and I remember looking up, searching for a sign to show me that his spirit had left his body, but I didn't see anything. He was such a stubborn man, and I often wonder whether he tried to take the stairs instead of the elevator to Heaven to prolong his stay here. I miss him dearly, think of him often, and his words still influence my life daily.

That man never took a single sick day off—ever. Until the day he received the news that he had cancer. That day, he left his workplace and never returned.

He worked as a general maintenance man at Thomas J. Lipton, the factory that makes soups and teas. There, he did a little bit of everything, including painting, concrete work and general repair. Every year, for three weeks in the summer, the Lipton plant shut down, and everyone went on holiday. Well, not everyone exactly. It was then that the company hired summer students to take care of little things around the factory that needed to be addressed. Usually, it was only the managers' kids who got these jobs, but my dad would get me in. This he did by offering a bottle of homemade wine to Marcel, a friendly Francophone shipping and receiving manager, and voilà . . . I had a summer job. At fourteen years old, my job was to load boxcars of Lipton Cup a Soup that would be delivered to Western Canada. While the full-time employee drove the forklift, two summer students were responsible for loading the boxcar, and it was an art. The procedure was to load one boxcar each day, half before lunch and the other half after. The boxes had to be stacked perfectly to the ceiling with no gaps in between to maximize the load. A fly couldn't have hitched a ride.

The shift started at seven a.m., but Dad liked arriving early to have coffee with his friends, and this meant my wake-up call was extra early at five thirty.

It was really hard work, and it was incredibly warm outside, so the morning after my very first day, I was lying in bed, sore from head to toe. My legs ached, my shoulders were sore, my back was stiff, and when I heard my dad approaching my room, I uttered while coming out of my sleep, "Papà, non credo che potrei andare a lavorare oggi. Sono stanco e molto dolorante. È estate e tutti i miei amici sono a casa." (Dad, I don't think I can go to work today. I'm tired and really sore. It's summer, and all of my friends are home.)

"Joseph, can you move your arms up and down?" he asked with what I now understand would have been a degree of sarcasm.

I strained while motioning my arms up and down.

"Can you reach out to the ceiling with both arms?" he continued.

Unbeknown to me at the time, I was making the same motions needed to load the boxcars successfully, and once he saw I was capable of this, his expression switched from empathetic to fierce. He grabbed my ear, pulled me out of bed and shouted, "Get the hell out of bed, you fagana sonamabetch! No son of mine is going to miss work today!"

It was then that he showed me his hands. I'd never paid attention to them before, and this was the first time that I really *looked* at them. They were rough, calloused, and his fingers were not entirely straight. As I looked at them, I wondered what they would say if they could speak. Dad softened his expression and said, "You don't want these hands, son. I did not come to this country so that you could have these hands. You want to carry a pencil, not a hammer. You want to wear a tie, not a uniform. You want to give orders, not take them from your boss like I do every morning. You want soft hands, son, not these hands."

My dad didn't want me to be him. He'd moved across the world to create a better life for his family, leaving his birthplace so that I'd have every opportunity to be the best I could be. The words he spoke that day have had a profound effect on my life, and they still influence my choices every single day.

I love my dad, and I always will, but he was right—I don't want his hands. Only you can determine what you want your hands to look like. The world thrives by having variety, and as long as your hands reflect your best self, all is good.

As a manager in a senior position, Who are you? was the first question I asked everyone I interviewed. By the time candidates got to me, Human Resources (HR) had already gone through a process of assessing their core competencies, education, skills and experience, so it was clear they could technically perform well in the position, but I wanted to know who they were. When asked this question, most candidates were stumped. They just weren't sure what to say, and mostly went on to describe their previous roles at places they'd worked. Essentially, they'd recite their resume, but I'd stop them and say, "I don't want to know what you did or what you will do when you're here. I want to know who you are." I wanted to know them as people, not employees.

I still ask that question but not just in job interviews. I ask it of most people I meet. If there is an opportunity to spend some time speaking with them, it's a great way to know people as people and also to have them begin to think about who they truly are. As conversation starters go, this is a good one.

It's also a great way to help people realize that the most important step toward being your best self is to understand who you truly are and to have complete self-awareness. Not of what you've done in life, but to understand truly, deeply and completely who you are. This isn't inspirational. It's foundational.

"What's your story?" I ask.

That's my follow-up question because we all have a story. It's the personal story of the journey through our physical and spiritual lives. Yes, most people are stumped again and not sure what to say. This time, I just let them tell me whatever they want to. Most begin with what they are doing in their work lives or what school they attend as students, but with a little bit of prodding, they soon begin to relay their story.

The Best Version of You

What does it mean to be your best self?

To simplify this, it means having complete self-awareness and understanding that each and every task you perform is to be done in a state of complete presence and to your maximum ability. Importance is no consideration. All things that you do are important. Your actions and efforts will affect how things eventually transpire.

Why strive to be your best self?

Becoming your best self is a journey on its own. It's one that will allow you to uncover, connect with, and clarify the true essence of who you are, what you're meant to do, and what stories will unfold throughout your life.

The path to becoming your best self is not linear. It contains many changes of direction, and the important thing is to continuously move forward. This is not one of those instances where you embark on the journey with the most direct and fastest route. For instance, let's imagine you want to walk around the world on foot. The fastest way to do so would be to travel in a straight line. Because the world is round, if you didn't veer right or left, eventually you'd end in the same place that you started. This is the most efficient way to journey around the world. It's also the way to learn the least about the world.

Instead of traveling in a straight line, I encourage you to take detours along the way. Ultimately, you'll still have traveled around the world and ended at your original starting point, but the learning experienced throughout your journey will be so much more enriching and rewarding. The sacrifice made is time, but it is time well spent, given the depth of the additional knowledge acquired.

Now, imagine doing this with every new discovery, and ask yourself, "How is it that I belong here?"

The answer will have a Multiplier Effect on all that you have learned throughout your journey.

As you turn the pages of this book, we're going to dive deeper into what the Multiplier Effect is. For now, the simplest way to get you acquainted with this term is to think of anything that enhances your experience. This includes thoughts and physical things.

Let's illustrate it with a few simple examples that serve as Multiplier Effects in my own life.

When I read, I always have a pencil in my hand. I call it my reading pencil, and I simply cannot concentrate as well without it. It boosts my reading experience just by holding it.

Meditating while contemplating decision paths is another example of a Multiplier Effect. The act of meditation allows me to make better decisions. Multiplier Effects can be grand and life-changing, as we'll discuss at length in later chapters, but they can also be small and simple.

Striving to be your best self is a lifelong endeavor. We learn as we go. Self-awareness and understanding of who we truly are fundamental to this process, and I'm committed to helping you get there by identifying what could be a Multiplier Effect to facilitate your journey of life, both professionally and personally. If this book has landed in your hands, it's no coincidence. It just means there is a part of you that yearns to be your best self.

So who are you, and what's your story? Jot something down below or on a separate notepad. You can always come back and write more later as you keep thinking about this.

_____

_____

_____

_____

_____

_____

_____

_____

_____

_____

_____

_____

_____

I'll ask you the same questions later in the book. You may describe who you are in the same way as you just did, or maybe that will change. We'll just have to wait and see how it evolves.

CHAPTER 2

The Multiplier Effect

The Multiplier Effect can be anything that supports you in achieving your best self and anything that enhances your experience of life. The key is that it's not one single thing. There are many things around you that can have that effect; some we're aware of and others we're not, but the possibilities are limitless.

To begin, here's what I need you to understand: Multiplier Effects can be ANYTHING. They are infinite. EVERYTHING has the possibility of having a positive effect in certain circumstances. They are personal and bespoke to each of us. Some have long-term effects. For example, education will have a Multiplier Effect on your long-term earning potential. Others will have a shorter-term effect, like using the correct shears to prune a rose bush, or a leaf blower instead of a rake to gather fallen leaves. What may be a Multiplier Effect for me may not be one for you, just as what may be one for you may not be one for your parents, husband, wife, sister, brother, or even a client. Don't compare your life or experiences to theirs because we all have a different mix of ingredients that make up who we are.

Here's a little story to compound the thinking . . .

I had my first paying job when I was twelve years old. It was at a private golf club, but the way it worked was slightly different from most jobs. Several times each week, my friends and I would arrive early at a designated section of the clubhouse. We'd sit on the benches and wait for the clubhouse attendant to come and select caddies for the members. If the attendant liked you, they'd pick you early. Some golfers had their preferred caddies, and if they were available at the right tee time, they were selected first. As with most things, there were grades: "AA" caddies, "A" caddies and "B" caddies. The AA's, who were the most knowledgeable about golf etiquette and the game in general, earned more and were usually selected first. The B's were the youngest and generally the least experienced. I was one of the B's. I waited until a member wanted a caddie of my caliber and hoped the attendant selected me. When he did, I'd carry the bag for five hours or so, and make $2.50 per eighteen holes. If the member was nice, he'd buy me a hot dog and a drink midway through the round. Not all were nice as some just ate their lunch in front of me while I waited. I hoped that one day I'd play golf just so I could select my own caddy and buy them lunch. Members who preferred B caddies were not the most proficient golfers, so the rounds took longer and required hawklike vision to find the array of unfortunate golf balls that regularly found their way into brush, forest and water. On a good day, I'd caddie for two rounds, one in the morning and one in the afternoon, and that earned me a cool $5.00. My friend Tony, who was built like a football linebacker even at that age, would carry two bags per round, earning twice as much as I did. Tony's strength was a Multiplier Effect on his ability to earn more money.

I didn't have the strength to carry two bags simultaneously, but I did have the option to earn more per golf round. All I needed to do was learn more about the game and demonstrate to the clubhouse attendant and golfers that I was capable of being an AA or A caddy. That way, I'd earn just as much as Tony by creating my own Multiplier Effect. Unfortunately, as I didn't have either the desire or the motivation to learn more about the game of golf, I didn't apply myself to put it into practice.

The purpose of a Multiplier Effect is to enhance your life. Can you pinpoint one for you at this very moment while reading this? Better lighting? A more comfortable seating position? Less background noises? If not, don't worry. By the end of this book, you'll be able to see them clearly.

There are things that have Multiplier Effects for many different scenarios, and that are long-term in nature. I call these Multi-Multipliers. For instance, you'll read about yoga in this book as it has been a Multi-Multiplier for me. One of my other favorites is salt. Yes, the humble mineral that has been used since ancient times for seasoning, preserving, disinfecting, and has even been used as an exchange unit. We can gargle with it to relieve a sore throat, use saline sprays for stuffy noses, soak our feet in salts and disinfect wounds with it. Salt serves a vital purpose in our bodies and maintains the proper functioning of muscles and nerves. If you add salt to a dish, you are seasoning it and making it better. It enhances flavor, giving your senses a better experience. Salt, with its multiple uses is a Multi-Multiplier.

The Diminishing Effect

Although the focus of this book is the Multiplier Effect, there are experiences and things we may do that will have the opposite effect in life and compromise our ability to be our best selves. I refer to them as the Diminishing Effects. If we spend our energy on the Multiplier Effect, the Diminishing Effect will become insignificant. If we know what they are, we can deal with them and identify a

Multiplier Effect to take their place. As a minimum, if we understand them, they will become temporary setbacks.

On occasion, there are lapses of judgment that defy comprehension and logic. Usually, it's a moment when we ask ourselves, "What in the world was I thinking?" These are the times that have temporary Diminishing Effects, but if we so choose, they can serve as catalysts for the Multiplier Effect. Having a temporary setback of some sort is normal and a part of life. It happens to all of us. Understanding what happened, learning from it and using it to launch into something positive is important—kind of like taking one step back in order to take two steps forward.

"The Story of the Supportive Spouse" is a good example of a Diminishing Effect. This came from a colleague who relayed a salary review process that was rather unusual. The employee whose salary was reviewed showed up at the scheduled meeting with his wife (who was not an employee of Standard Life). He apparently just sat down while she did most of the talking! He did not get a raise and the experience affected his reputation among his peers and in the company.

This certainly had a Diminishing Effect on his advancement in the company. Wouldn't you agree?

Think of something that has had a Diminishing Effect on you. Write it down.

_____

_____

_____

_____

_____

_____

How did you respond to this?

Was it an opportunity to open a new door and improve? Was it something that had lingering negative effects?

If something is currently having a Diminishing Effect on you, how are you going to react?

For those of you whose mind is now jumping ahead and thinking, "How will I know what a Diminishing Effect for me is?" Don't worry. Focus on the Multiplier Effects, and the rest will fall into place naturally. Trust me.

That leads us to one of the most important Multiplier Effects—spirituality.

CHAPTER 3

Happiness and Joyfulness

Materialism and spirituality can happily coexist within each of us and having material possessions is not a bad thing. I enjoy having nice things, and they bring me happiness. There is a practical element to material things—we need them. Striving for possessions is a good thing—it means we'll be rewarded for our efforts, and that will make us happy. Being spiritually awakened is a joyful state. However, being joyful and enjoying the results of your efforts from a material perspective are not mutually exclusive. If you work hard, acquire what you have legally and ethically and are open to sharing with the world, it is yours to enjoy. You can have the beautiful house, the beautiful car, enjoy a glass of wine on occasion and still be spiritually awakened. There is no separation between that and being in a state of best self from a materialistic perspective.

You don't need to select between being a spiritual or material human being. Taken to the extremes, they are diametrically opposed. Striving to be in a constant state of bliss is noble but not practical and being driven to succeed is materialistic and leads to selfishness and unhappiness. Doing unethical or illegal things, which is often the result of an unbridled ambition to succeed materialistically, is not noble or practical either. But it is possible to be a pleasant blend of both. As a matter of fact, being both is the only way to achieve your best self. The benefits and balance of being spiritual will enhance all of your senses and awareness and result in your ability to perform consistently at a higher level. If you blend meditation and spiritual awakening into your daily life, professional or otherwise, everything you do will be enhanced.

You'll be more productive in business, more effective as leaders and perform better in sports. You'll become better friends, partners and parents, and it will truly complement your ability to reach your full potential.

One of the beautiful things that will happen as you embark on your personal journey toward being your best self is the effect that you'll have on others. You will, in fact, become a part of their journey as they move toward achieving their best self because we each have an important role to play in the construct of rising to greatness. One significant component of achieving your best self is to understand what you can do to contribute toward helping others achieve the same. Helping them will help you achieve yours, and not many things in life can be as satisfying as this. Did I just imply that the positive energy pouring out of you when helping others circles back to help you and thus serves as a Multiplier Effect itself? Yes, I did. Wow, how cool is that?

Spirituality has a Multiplier Effect on our ability to achieve our highest level. This then has a ripple effect on how we show up for others and shows the capacity in which we can contribute to their lives.

Remember, this is an ongoing journey, not a final destination. Incorporating spirituality into your journey will allow you to remain present and feel joy and happiness in pursuit of reaching your best self.

Being your best self does not strictly mean maximizing your

success in the professional work environment. The spiritual element of personal growth is the second half that makes you whole. As you continue reading, extract the teachings that resonate with you based on the stories and suggestions; my hope is that you will understand that being your best self is a combination of both practical and spiritual things. The Multiplier Effect of spirituality complements our experiences and follows us into every area of our lives.

It could be argued that while joyfulness occurs when you are completely self-aware of who you are, why you are and how you are, happiness is relative and is based on different things for different people. Unfortunately, for many, it is based on a multitude of different things that are often materialistic, like money, music, cars and travel.... I've observed that the happiness experienced by those external factors is short-lived. Then those attracted to this kind of happiness move quickly on to something else or want a new-and-improved version of what they just experienced. We have an insatiable appetite to drive toward what we perceive as happiness, but we never seem to achieve it or, if we do, sustain it. When we rely on externally driven circumstances to make us happy, we are giving away our right to what makes us happy by outsourcing it to other people and things.

When you are joyful, you understand your purpose and your right to exist in this universe. You are also at peace with yourself and your place in the world. You don't necessarily need anything to make you joyful. It is completely internally driven and completely within your control.

Being joyful is more consistent than being happy because it's cultivated and created internally. This joyfulness comes when you examine yourself from within and truly understand who you are, what your place is in this world and why you are here. It's spiritual. Joyfulness is a choice, and where happiness has a shelf life, joyfulness does not.

Without a dictionary, define what happiness and joyfulness mean to you.

Pause your reading, grab a pen and paper, and then take a few moments to reflect.

Write out what makes you happy.
Write out what makes you joyful.

Happy

Joyful

_____

_____

_____

_____

_____

_____

If you conclude that similar things make you both happy and joyful, you're thinking exactly as I was several years ago. I'd have responded that a great career, a loving family and financial independence were the three things that made me both happy and joyful. I now realize that this is only half of what would truly make me both.

Can you be happy and joyful at the same time? Absolutely. I wish I'd known the difference when I was pursuing a career in my corporate life. I would not only have been fortunate to achieve the things that I did, but I would also have been joyful doing so. If you're joyful and happy, you'll achieve your best self, and a world of possibilities will open up to you.

Love me or love me not?
Tears of happiness or tears of joy
are your choice.

Remember, joyfulness is our end goal, and we're going to be happy getting there.

CHAPTER 4

Laws to Live By

Even though I don't believe in sheer luck, I do believe that I have a guardian angel who has follows me around, looking out for me. I've been so fortunate in life that I can't believe otherwise. Have you ever had situations where you just can't believe what happened to you? Maybe you've heard yourself say, "What are the chances of that?"

I've said that to myself many times throughout my personal and professional life, and I remember one particular time as if it were yesterday . . .

I was fourteen years old and on my way home from school. I had to take two buses, which included a transfer, and if the buses were on time and traffic was in my favor, the wait for the transfer from one bus to the other was approximately ten minutes. To get to the bus stop, I had to cross a very busy intersection, and on that day, traffic was light, which usually meant the cars were driving faster. My second bus was early because I could see my transfer bus as I got off the first one. The traffic light was red, and I'm not sure why, but I decided that it was a good idea to run through the red light before it turned green, in the hope of making the bus. I didn't see the car coming. As I was halfway across the road, singularly focused on getting on that bus, it was suddenly as if someone reached out and grabbed me by the shoulder. I stopped in my tracks. In that exact moment, a car, inches from me, shaved past, and if I'd taken one more step, I would have been hit by it. I was shocked. When I looked around to see whether someone had put their hand on my shoulder, there was no one there. That day, I may have missed my bus, but more importantly, I missed a trip to the hospital and quite possibly to the cemetery.

Although I consider myself to be very fortunate generally, I don't necessarily believe in luck. Nor do I believe in coincidences. What I do believe in are the Twelve Laws of Karma. Everything happens for a reason, and we influence what happens with our actions and thoughts. Those thoughts and actions create opportunities, and I first became aware of these laws when I learned more about the spiritual discipline of yoga.

As one awakens spiritually, one realizes that most of the world is asleep.

Here is a quick synopsis to help you understand their basic elements:

Cause and Effect: This law is also sometimes referred to as the Great Law and is one of the most universally understood laws of karma. Have you heard the saying "You get what you give", which summarizes this law? If you give something positive, something positive will happen to you in return. Conversely, if you do something negative, something negative will also happen to you in return.

Creation: I sometimes refer to this as the law of impatience. As the name suggests, we shouldn't wait for something to happen; we should act to make it happen. Just taking a course, applying for a job or asking that special person for a first date can make a big difference in your life.

Humility: Being present and having self-awareness will help you accept things that currently exist in your life. I believe that I am currently in my circumstance because of everything that I've said and done in my life to date. Understanding this helps me to recognize why I am in such a place.

Growth: I love this law! It is all about knowing yourself and continuing on your path to personal growth. It begins internally and expands externally. This law is essential to achieving your maximum potential and is a primary focus for this book.

Responsibility: I sometimes refer to this law in conjunction with the Law of Humility. It suggests that you are where you are in your life because of your actions and words, and therefore you are responsible for being in your current state. Understand that you have made your own bed, and it is up to you whether you are happy sleeping in it.

Connection: Another one of my favorite laws! One way or another, all things and all people are connected as we are all part of one universe. We all work together in harmony. This concept applies to all time—past, present and future. I am constantly trying to do things today to change the consequences of what happened in the past. A simple example is apologizing to someone for something that you said or did that offended them.

Focus: At one time, I prided myself on my ability to multitask. The more things on the go, the better! I now realize that this is rubbish. We can't possibly be at our best for any given task if we divide our attention and thoughts on multiple things. Have you, like me, tried to do something while thinking of something else? We devote an entire chapter in this book to this law.

Giving and Hospitality: As per the Law of Connection, we are all connected in some way. This makes us responsible for each other and all living things. It is not just a concept or something that we speak about—it is important, for the good of all, that we action our sense of responsibility. We should give back to our communities and each other.

Here and Now: This law speaks about being present at all times. Do you know of someone who seems to be living and reliving their past? Have you noticed how it has affected their present? We don't want to be there. It's important to remember and acknowledge the past, but not live in it. We should understand what could lie in the future but not at the expense of losing awareness of our present. I personally have a slightly different view about this one, as I'll explain in Chapter 14.

Change: We need to be in a constant state of change in order to keep moving forward as human beings. The universe will provide whatever you need, but the key is to acknowledge that a change is necessary to progress. Don't be proud or stubborn, accept the fact that change is constant and embracing it will make you better.

Patience and Reward: Work hard, trust the process and be patient. Success will follow. We cover this law extensively in the book. There is no substitute for hard work.

Significance and Inspiration: Do not underestimate your ability to make a difference in the world. We all have something of value to share with the universe, and every time we do, large or small, we make the world a better place.

These are summarized as the Laws of Karma, but in reality, many of them are found in different cultures and belief systems in a roundabout way. They are not unique to one country, population or culture. They are universal laws.

Looking back, I've inadvertently abided by a few of the Laws of Karma and the Law of Focus serves as an excellent example. Having always been able to prioritize, my energy was expended on what I believed to be the most important at that particular time. I had, and still have, a laser focus when I decide what I want to do next. My wife Mary summed it up best when I announced that I was going to write a book. She asked, "Have you absolutely decided to write a book?" I told her yes, and she just smiled and said, "All right then, once you've decided to do something, it's best to just step back and get out of your way. Write your book."

Understanding the Laws of Karma has accelerated my ability toward achieving the ultimate goal—to be my best always. Had I known and understood all these laws earlier in my life and career, I'm convinced that my path toward happiness and joy would have had fewer bumps and obstacles.

I believe that understanding and following these laws will lead to a clear path toward maximizing your ability and potential as a human being. This, in turn, will lead to you achieving what you desire in life on all levels—personally, professionally and spiritually.

When there is no hope, there is hurt.
Among the ashes of hurt, like the
phoenix, clarity will arise.
With clarity, there is hope.

Clarity Through Yoga and Meditation

The attraction to yoga was natural for me and has been an important part of my life for many years. I initially became interested in it as a physical means to treat chronic back pain, something I'd experienced for years. As I learned more, I became more interested. This was the beginning of my journey to becoming a yoga teacher. The word *yoga* itself means union—the union of the individual spirit with the spirit of a higher being. It helps you to exist in harmony with your own mind, body and environment. This is a path to achieving your best self.

There are countless texts and sources of information that describe yoga, and my preferred source is *The Yoga-Sutra of Patañjali*. By collecting and organizing ancient knowledge of yoga, Patañjali explains its theory and the practice in 196 aphorisms. You may be familiar with Patañjali's Eight Limbs of Yoga. In that, he summarizes eight steps that begin externally and end internally, with their purpose being how to live a meaningful and purposeful life. All of the elements are important, and the asanas, the physical component described as the third limb, are perhaps the most commonly known in the Western world. I consider dhyana meditation, represented by the seventh limb, very important to my continued well-being and journey toward becoming my best self, and I would encourage you to learn about yoga to help you become the best person you can be.

There are many types of meditation. For ease of reference, I will briefly outline the six most popular, but only you can decide which is best for you.

Focused Meditation

This is one of my favorite forms of meditation. While sitting or lying down, I focus on my breath coming in and out of my body, although focus can be placed on any of our five senses. Sometimes I will keep my eyes open and focus on a flame or fireplace, and at other times, if accessible, I stare at a body of water. I recommend mala beads to some of my students who have a difficult time quieting their minds. This way, their focus is on moving through the beads.

Mantra Meditation

Sit in a comfortable position, close your eyes and choose a word or phrase that works for you to continuously repeat. This serves as your mantra and it should be something soothing. A couple of popular examples include "Om" and "I am that I am". I personally find "Om" magical!

Mindfulness Meditation

We cannot control our thoughts; therefore, it's important to acknowledge them for what they are—just thoughts. I teach this type of meditation to most of my students because it's relatively simple to do. Most say that they've tried meditation but just can't "focus on nothing." "How do I empty my mind?" they ask. I think that most are just impatient. Once they sit in a comfortable position and *just be for a little while, even just* a few moments, they begin to understand the magic of mindfulness meditation.

Movement Meditation

The yoga asanas! Participating in a yoga class and focusing on your breath and movement is a popular and excellent way of practicing movement meditation. I've taught classes where the yogis all moved in perfect sync with their breath for a full hour of a Vinyasa flow. Just a sea of people moving in alignment together, almost trancelike. It was magical. Other forms of movement meditation include any form of gentle movement, including walking.

Transcendental Meditation

This is in many ways very similar to a mantra meditation, but the mantra word or phrase is specifically suited for you and usually reflects a specific intention. Some examples could be "I am health," "I am wealth" or "I am worthy." I personally use "I am health, I am wealth, I am yoga".

Spiritual Meditation

As the name implies, this meditation refers to a connection with God and can be practiced anywhere, especially in places of worship.

I meditate to help quiet my mind. We live in a world with a seemingly infinite number of mediums to access information. This is fantastic. Unfortunately, we're also bombarded with information on a consistent basis from all of these different mediums. We now have new terms like *fake news* and *alternative facts*, and this is an outright assault on our intelligence. The sheer volume of information and misinformation that is available is enormous, but the quality, its source and accuracy are always to be questioned.

Within this environment, we're required to make hundreds of decisions each day, many of which need to be instant. Some will be minor (what bus route shall I take home tonight?), and some will be major (should I put an offer down on a house?). Some will be personal (what am I having for dinner tonight?), and some will be professional (should I mention my frustration to my boss?). Making the wrong decision at any given time can have a significant effect on your personal and professional life. Yet we often need to make these decisions quickly and repeatedly, hoping for the best. Having a clear mind helps us to make better decisions and achieve optimal performance. The ability to quickly sift through information that is available, decide what is applicable to each circumstance and apply it to the decision-making process is more critical than ever.

There are countless credible studies supporting the numerous benefits of meditation. All of them help to maintain a healthy mental state. In my opinion, helping to quiet and clear your mind is the most important feature of consistent meditation.

I meditate as part of my personal well-being. The benefits are scientifically documented and numerous, and while there are many more benefits than these, meditation can:
- Control stress
- Promote emotional health
- Increase attention span
- Help with memory loss
- Help improve sleep
- Help to decrease blood pressure
- Help to increase self-awareness

It gets better too. Meditation has also helped me think through many important situations and issues more clearly, and that has resulted in better conclusions and action plans. If you think about it, that makes sense. Meditation does not clear your mind. Your brain doesn't work that way. If you ask yourself to stop thinking about something, what usually happens? You start thinking about it even more. You can't just say, "Whatever thoughts are in my mind, I order them to disappear."

What meditation actually does is help you accept the thoughts that come and go in your mind. It helps rid your mind of its clutter, and this, in turn, helps you to think more clearly. When I have an important decision to make, a problem to solve or any issue to resolve, I meditate on it.

The Laws of Karma, as explained above or your personal version and interpretation of them, are real. Take a look at them again and understand that all of them are important. Which ones particularly resonate with you?

Now, take a look at the various types of meditation described above. Which one(s) would be interesting for you to try?

CHAPTER 5

There is No Substitute for Hard Work

I love the word *work*. It's a great word, and it has an enormous Multiplier Effect on your ability to succeed.

Working hard is the minimum requirement if you want to achieve your best. No one has ever coasted to greatness. If you're not willing to work hard and consistently give your maximum effort, you'll never achieve the results you're capable of. Work forms an integral part of the fabric of our society, and it's associated with good things. It contributes to our sense of well-being and accomplishment, proves our ability to provide and boosts our self-esteem. I love work.

You may be thinking, "Working hard is good, but if I work smarter, I won't have to work as hard." Fair enough, but if you want to achieve greatness, you must always do both. I prefer the person who has a strong work ethic over someone with the ability to figure out a way to work smarter but less. You can't teach work ethic, but you can teach someone to work smarter.

The one who self-promotes harder than they work will be known more for their self-promotion than their work.

Why Do We Do What We Do?

We act out of desire. When we desire something, we act accordingly. Desire is made out of what we want, and what we should always want is to achieve the best possible outcome. Anything less is to compromise our path toward achieving our best self. Let me explain that in a little more detail . . .

Desiring a mediocre result should never be acceptable—settling for "good enough" is never good enough. That is a poor excuse to not expend the energy and effort to work toward excellence. It's the lazy person's way of working, and it leads to being less than 100 percent of what you should be, optimally.

Normally, we desire things that are linked to pleasure, things that are pleasurable and make us happy. Sometimes our desire is to accomplish something because of an event that happened in our lives that had a profound impact on us. Or maybe it's driven by something we want deeply, like a dream job that will give us the abundance we seek as well as the ability to transform our lives. It may simply be a case of wanting to be like someone we admire, like wearing the same hairstyle as a favorite celebrity. So what do you desire?

- To own a specific home or car?
- To help find a cure for something?

- To build schools in a third-world country?
- To find love?
- To live free of stress?

Let's consider an example. If you desire deep love and connection, you'll be motivated and won't settle for just anyone as a partner. You'll work on personal development because you'll remember that how you showed up in your past relationships may not have served you well. You'll do your best to put your best foot forward to impress the one that captures your heart.

Why do we sometimes need something or someone to kickstart the process of achieving what we desire? It's because we have a desire buried deep inside of us, and it needs to be awakened. Other times, when we truly desire something, it's natural to be drawn to it, and we don't need an event to mobilize ourselves into action. However, desire itself is not enough.

Desire without motivation is simply an idea that lingers within the confines of possibility. This compromises happiness. Motivation is the *why* and the reason for actioning your desire.

What do you desire?

_____

_____

_____

What is your motivation?

_____

_____

_____

_____

If your unwavering and constant desire is striving to always be the best possible version of yourself, your motivation is clear, and you'll have boundless energy to reach a level of maximum joyfulness and happiness. Remember, this is our ultimate goal.

Now, let's circle back to work ethic. Motivation helps drive a strong work ethic. People naturally work harder when they're motivated to do something. Therefore, a strong work ethic is the Multiplier Effect. This will drive your behavior to do what's required of you to achieve the desired outcome of being your best self.

Our minds are like the ocean.
The deeper you delve,
the more fascinating the findings.

The 100% Rule

It is important to do everything at 100 percent maximum effort, no matter how large or small the task. Otherwise, it's a slippery slope when we begin to pick and choose which tasks are worthy of greater effort. Remember, we don't want to settle for "good enough." Your perception of something important can be vastly different from someone else's perception of the same thing, and this applies in your personal and professional life. Imagine you have a friend looking for a job who asks for help with editing their resume. What would happen to your friendship if you showed little interest and only briefly glanced at it, commenting that "it's good enough"? But how would your friend react if you took the time to properly edit the resume with a genuine interest in helping them? Let's look at a similar example in the workplace.

Imagine a colleague asks for your opinion on a presentation that they'll be giving that afternoon, and it's very important to them that everything goes well. The presentation will take up time and has nothing to do with your job or department. What would you do? Would you glance at it and say it was fine, or would you take the time to carefully look at it? Would you go one step further and sacrifice your lunch hour so your colleague could practice their presentation and you could give useful feedback? Your response here will determine the type of relationship you two will have moving forward. If you decide to help, focus all of your attention on the task at hand because, in that moment, it is the most important thing there is. Nothing else matters or exists. Your understanding of this is the Multiplier Effect that will help you achieve greatness in each and every moment.

Do you remember a time when you stopped at "good enough"? You may think, *Of course I have. I never have time to do everything that needs to be done, so most of the time I stop at good enough.* Since when is "good enough" good enough?

Giving 100 percent effort does not mean performing at 100 percent peak efficiency at all times, which is impossible, it means doing everything you can to be at your best at any given time. Think about that. If, for some reason, your energetic capacity is only 80 percent, you're still obligated to give 100 percent effort to that 80 percent you're capable of at that moment. Let's use a hockey player as an example. If, prior to a game, one of the players has a hamstring strain and is still able to play, they can still give 100 percent even if their capacity is temporarily diminished due to the strain. If that player focuses on giving 100 percent of the effort they have available, they'll be satisfied with themselves because they provided their maximum effort under not-so-ideal circumstances.

Working hard and giving your best effort will always lead to better results, and you'll have a greater chance at success in everything you do. Employers, coaches and teachers will notice. Friends, family and lovers will notice. Opportunities will be abundant because people want to be around people who are not only *at* their best but have standardized *giving* their best, regardless of their current life situation. Is this something that inspires and motivates you?

Hard Work vs Talent

Hard work with less talent will always triumph over talent that is not willing to work hard. We see examples of this all around us. Do you know of anyone who you wish would work a little bit harder or put more effort in because you know that they can do so much more? Those of us with children understand that all too well! You may even see it in yourself. If so, snap out of it. Refer back to the 100 Percent Rule if you need to. Don't be selfish about it because it's not just about you but everything and everyone around you. Keep reading if you want to make sure this doesn't happen again.

I believe people who don't work to be their best selves are doing a disservice to themselves, their friends, families, coworkers and society in general. I strongly believe that we all have an obligation to achieve the most we are capable of. I was, and to a certain degree still am, a very competitive person. While I want everyone to do well, I still need to do better. This competitive nature has softened somewhat over the years, but it's still there. It's one of the drivers that motivates me to work hard, and I don't have an issue with failing at anything or losing a competition to someone if I know that I have given 100 percent in effort. I can live with the loss. Having said that, 100 percent effort doesn't mean just working hard at a specific task. It also means doing all of the proper preparation beforehand.

You can give 100 percent effort to a task, but if you don't prepare properly, you'll fail. I've heard many people justify failures by suggesting that they gave their all and it wasn't good enough. This may be true, but if they didn't give 100 percent effort to the process and they ignored what was required in terms of the preparation to do well, failure was inevitable.

Athletes who perform at a high level provide a great illustration, and many of them share common traits. They certainly have God-given physical talent, a work ethic that is extraordinary, and they practice relentlessly, always looking for ways to improve themselves. These people work on the physical and mental aspects of their craft. They care about nutrition and are keenly aware of the workings of their bodies. But that's not all—they have the ability to focus with incredible intensity and are meticulous in their preparation for competition. Excellent examples are: Michael Jordan, LeBron James, Tom Brady, Usain Bolt, Lionel Messi, Serena Williams and Lewis Hamiltion. Michael Jordan, in his prime, was a sight to behold. Some would argue that he willed his team to win and refused to lose, but that isn't the case. What he did was match the intensity of his physical effort to his mental effort. If the two are in sync, anything is possible. One of the problems most of us face is that the two efforts are not in sync as often as they could or should be. We often feel great physically, but our mental attitude is not there; our minds are ready, but we haven't done the physical work for the task at hand. Michael Jordan never had this issue. Mind and body always worked as one. The two halves, physically and mentally aligned, made for a much greater whole.

The Mind and Body as One

I encourage you to examine your life as it is, in this very instant, and to understand that you are capable of achieving much more than you think.

Our minds are not potentially capable of extraordinary things but are capable of achieving the extraordinary. If we shift our thinking from what we believe is possible to what is absolutely attainable, we begin to relieve ourselves of the self-imposed shackles that prevent us from being our best.

While our minds have unlimited capacity, our bodies do not. We're physically limited by our height, strength, flexibility, bone structure, genetics and a host of other things. Each of us is different from a physical perspective, and each of us has unique limitations. These are physical boundaries, and we need to understand our bodies' limitations. Only with this understanding can we realize our unique capabilities.

The unlimited potential of your mind will help you to realize the maximum potential of your body, and it's only when the two are totally in alignment that you'll be able to achieve your best self.

We don't need to be high-level athletes or top performers to apply the same principles. Each of us can put into practice an approach that is bespoke and appropriate for ourselves.

What Are You Proud Of?

Being proud of the results of your efforts will make you work harder.

How often have you heard someone say that they are proud of their work? How about the company they work for? We tell our kids that we are proud of them. We are proud of someone's effort, proud of making a brave decision, proud of our heritage and our country . . . but our work? I don't hear that much anymore. These days, people are quick to change jobs, and there is less of a sense of loyalty to a company than there was in the past. Everyone should be proud of their effort and their work, and they should look for an employer who they can be proud of. Each of us will have criteria of what we're looking for in an employer we'd be proud of working for. Equal opportunity, diversification of staff, fair and equal wages and commitment to the environment would be some of mine. And what about the kind of work the company itself does? I wouldn't want to work for a company that had all of these things but was in an industry that I didn't respect. Working for an employer that you can be proud of is something to consider when looking for opportunities to be your best self. You'll not only be happier because of it, but you'll work harder for it.

Pause your reading to reflect. What are you proud of and why?

_____

_____

_____

_____

_____

_____

_____

_____

_____

_____

_____

_____

_____

A Sense of Pride

One day, when I returned home from the office, my youngest son, Samuel, asked me an interesting question. He said, "Dad, what do you do?"

"What do you mean? I'm the President of Standard Life," I replied.

He told me then that he knew that, but he still wanted to know exactly what that meant. How do you explain to your nine-year-old son what a president of an insurance company does? I thought about it for a while and came up with an answer:

"Daddy has a lot of friends at Standard Life, and they help many people. When someone becomes sick while on vacation, we help them see a doctor and give them medicine. We help them come back home quickly. When someone needs braces, we help them get a dentist. We also help people who are working to save some of their money so that they can buy nice gifts for their grandchildren when they retire, like Nonna, your grandmother. We are an important company, and we help a lot of people."

At this, Samuel nodded and asked a follow-up question, "Dad, are you proud of Standard Life?" I never really thought about it before, but it was so obvious. "Yes, I am. I am very proud of Standard Life and all of my friends there," I said.

It was true. I was very proud of Standard Life but never really talked about it. It occurred to me then that we don't often think about our employers as being places that create a sense of pride. This is different from what I had grown up with. My dad was very proud of his company and his work. He gave me a tour of the Lipton plant, saying, "Do you see that wall, Joseph? That's my wall. I had to repair it, and it took over a day because the symmetry was off, but I did it." Then he continued, "Do you see that tank container? That's my tank. I had to weld a fault behind it. It was less than one foot from the wall. I wrenched my back, but I did it."

It was not just my dad who was proud. My father-in-law was too. He was a construction worker who specialized in cement finish, and he worked on Terminal 3 of Toronto Pearson International Airport when it was being constructed. Specifically, he worked on the cement pillars in Terminal 3, and each time I traveled, he reminded me of those pillars because he was proud of them. When you look for a job, select it and the company with a sense of future pride. When you're proud of your company and your work, it drives you to do your best.

Busy, Busy, Busy

As a teenager, my agenda was always full and I kept a scheduler that was also always full. Being organized and knowing what to do next was very important to me. It was also important to check off each item once completed, every day. When I was in high school, my calendar held my class schedule and my practice and game schedule for whatever sport I was into at the time. It also included the amount of time allocated for homework before and after dinner, and finally, which TV shows to watch in the evening. These were the only items listed during the week, but weekends were usually open. Each night, just before going to bed, I'd look at my calendar and make sure each item on it had been completed. This gave me a sense of accomplishment and satisfaction. I kept up this habit, and I feel that it's important, at the end of each day, to reflect on what you set out to achieve and what you've accomplished. Reflecting on your daily accomplishments gives you a sense of satisfaction and time well spent.

As I moved into my late teenage years, I wondered how much we could accomplish if we didn't sleep as much as we do. Imagine all of the extra things we could do if we had an extra few hours or so in the day? During university, I slept very little, and this worked for a while, but I soon realized my body required a certain amount of sleep to keep up with my busy schedule. Understanding how much sleep you need is important and one of your key Multiplier Effects. I attended classes, studied in the library and spent time with friends. I earned pocket money by selling shoes on Friday nights and Saturdays. Sundays were for studying. This was how I lived for years, always up for having fun but never allowing my schoolwork to be compromised because I knew that education had a Multiplier Effect on my future success.

Sleep, of course, is important for our overall well-being and good health, and I'm constantly calculating the minimum number of hours I need each night to perform my very best the next day.

When I was senior vice president at Standard Life, my residence was in Oakville, but I was required to be in Montreal three days each week. I'd spend Mondays and Fridays in our Toronto office and Tuesdays, Wednesdays and Thursdays in Montreal, and despite the travel, I was incredibly productive. During those weekdays in Montreal, my working day began at seven a.m. and ended at approximately eight p.m. With my family being back in Oakville, I had no particular place to go, and so I stayed late in the evenings to prepare for meetings the next day. I'd also catch up on reading reports and so on. The office was relatively quiet after five p.m., and any work done after that was, for the most part, completely uninterrupted. I find that three hours of uninterrupted work is the equivalent of six hours of work during regular working hours. Although the time away from my family was difficult, from a professional perspective, I viewed this schedule as advantageous for me. I worked nearly a full week in terms of hours between Tuesday and Thursday, and Mondays and Fridays were bonus workdays.

This attitude applied to weekends as well. If there was office work to be done on the weekend, it was done, and I was always available to my colleagues. Most exchanges were handled by email, and if I required something, or someone required something from me, it was taken care of. I understand the concept and importance of work/ life balance clearly. The key is to be present when required to be so, something that is discussed at length in Chapter 14. However, if you decide that weekends are absolutely not for work and maintain that view, it will undermine your professional opportunities. There will always be times when you'll be needed beyond regular office hours, and leaders will turn to people who are willing to work when required. You want to facilitate avenues for success, not restrict them. Creating boundaries such as strict work hours will create restrictions on your ability to succeed.

As president and CEO of Standard Life, I was required to attend executive meetings in Scotland on a monthly basis. My flight schedule began each Sunday morning, flying from Montreal to Toronto, Toronto to London with a stay overnight at Heathrow Airport. I'd then take the earliest flight from London to Edinburgh on Monday morning. During that time, I took advantage of the long flight overseas to read the more than one hundred pages of reports that would prepare me for upcoming meetings. I'd make a list of questions for whoever I needed the information from in Canada. This was usually our CFO, Christian Martineau. Once I got to Heathrow Airport, I emailed my questions, and by the time I was ready for my Monday morning flight to Edinburgh, Christian had already responded. He was the Multiplier Effect that helped me be my best when representing our Canadian division. And he worked on weekends more often than not.

I often hear "I do not work on weekends," or "Anything can wait until Monday." This is not the way we should think. Sometimes, you have to work when you have to work.

I believe that every day is whatever you wish to make it—a workday, a family day or any other type of day. They are just days to be occupied by whatever is required from a pleasure, personal or professional perspective. Don't worry what day of the week it is, just identify the Multiplier Effects that will help you continue your path toward becoming your best self.

My parents taught me that keeping busy doing what you love, and sometimes doing what you don't love but what is necessary, will always lead to good things.

Being idle is next to impossible in today's world, so choose what is important and get on with it.

Time Is Our Most Valuable Resource

Today, I view time as everyone's most valuable currency. Each second of each minute should be taken with great seriousness and valued with the utmost importance and respect. We are given a finite number of minutes, and we have no idea how many that will be. Whenever I consider doing anything, I don't ask myself whether it's worth ten dollars or a hundred. I ask whether it's worth the time it will take away from my personal time allocation. Is standing in line for an hour worth an hour of my life? Perhaps it is, and perhaps it's not. These days, I always ask the question, *Is it worth my time?* Because it's not just time that is ticking away . . . it's the limited amount of time that has been allocated for your life.

If you're like me, you get bored every so often—at least I think I'm bored. When this happens, I try to catch those drifting thoughts about being bored or knowing I soon will be if I do something in particular. There really is no excuse for boredom because there is always something to do that will occupy your time in a productive manner. People who are bored are people who are unable to be in the moment and experience life as it exists in time. Being bored means that, for some reason, you're not in a happy state, let alone a joyful one. Time is too valuable to be bored.

Think about when you are most often bored. Is it when you are alone? At work or school? When doing a particular thing or speaking to a certain person? There are many things it could be, so look for clues, think about it and write your thoughts down.

I'm most bored when:

_____

_____

_____

_____

_____

_____

_____

_____

_____

_____

_____

_____

Think about what you can do to change the narrative of being bored when you are experiencing the same things that you wrote above.

Now, let's make a deal together. Let's NEVER think about being bored again.

Work hard. Give 100 percent effort always. Understand your desire and what motivates you. Be proud of your work. Do not acknowledge boredom. Align the mind and body, and if you do these things, is it really work?

You are on your way. Magic will follow.

CHAPTER 6

Hardly Working

One evening in Montreal, I was having dinner with Sandy, our Group Chief Executive at Standard Life. Sandy was regularly in town for meetings, and we usually found time to meet up to discuss the day's events and the next day's schedule. Often, our discussions veered in a more personal direction, and on occasion, the topic turned to our children. Mine were still quite young, and one day, I told him about my life plan for them: postsecondary education being a certainty. They were going to have good values, good hygiene and good grooming habits, which are a must. They'd also have clean rooms and most definitely white-collar jobs. It didn't end there though. My plan included them playing sports throughout their childhood, and when they got older, they were going to date well-educated and respectful people from good families, and there would be absolutely no drugs or alcohol!

I carried on, explaining to Sandy how frustrated I was when they didn't do their homework or their chores, and because of that, I felt my plan for them might be in jeopardy. In retrospect, I was micromanaging my kids, something I'd never have stood for from my parents. After listening to my rambling, he smiled and told me to stop making them what I wanted them to be. There were going to turn out to be who they were supposed to be anyway. Sandy was wise.

We're all blessed with a certain mix of ingredients at birth, and I believe that all human beings form a higher consciousness. Thus, we're all intricately linked at a higher level, and because of this, we owe it to ourselves, society, the world and the universe to maximize our ability and become the best we can be. If we share both a higher consciousness and the planet, we need to be respectful of our role in the universe.

The most important part of maximizing our potential is to understand who we are as individuals. We need to stop worrying about who we are *not* and focus on discovering who we really are. This is fundamental if we want to achieve joy, happiness and success, because too often we believe we are what others believe we should be.

No one has the right to dictate the type of person you should become, but everyone seems to have an opinion. If you allow these opinions into your heart, your happiness and joyfulness will be compromised.

As children, we're naturally happy, and we don't need anything to make us so. We play with toys, and we're amused by the sheer discovery of our surroundings. But then, as we grow, something happens to us, and we need external stimulation to make us happy. Something to amuse us. Then, we're told how to be amused. When you give a child a toy, they often play with the wrapping because maybe they find the colorful packaging interesting. When they do that, we adults tell them how to play with the toy instead. Where is the logic in that? If we give a child a toy and they play with the box, why are we then so quick to point out that it's not the box that provides the fun factor? Why does it have to be the actual toy itself? What if the child is perfectly happy playing with the box or packaging? Who are we to determine what should make them happy? As children, we are constantly being told what to do, how to act and who to be. This is a suppression of the natural joy and unlimited curiosity children are born with.

As we move along into adulthood, too often we are reminded of who we are or who we are not, but that's down to nobody but ourselves to decide.

Do any of the following sound familiar to you?

- You are not like her. She achieved good grades and is now very successful.
- You are just like him. He never amounted to much.
- You are such a troublemaker.
- You ask too many questions, just listen for a change.
- Why can't you be more like . . .
- You are not enough . . .

This is all nonsense. Who you are not doesn't matter. Who you are is important.

Discover Your Ideal Career

As an executive coach and yoga teacher, I've helped counsel many people about career choices and career changes. During this process, I discovered key elements that helped me steer people into careers that were ideally suited to them. In many cases, we uncovered career opportunities that they'd never even considered, and mostly, our discussions turned to what they were passionate about. I'm certain you've heard the saying, "It's not work if you love what you are doing." That's because people are naturally drawn to what they're passionate about.

An ideal career choice stems from having self-awareness and knowing how to link who you are to a career that will bring out the best in you. A simple exercise that I use to bridge the two together is to ask a series of questions. So, I'm asking that of you now. Think about them, and then write down your answers:

What do I like about myself?
What do I love about myself?
What do I dislike about myself?
What do I despise about myself?
What am I good at?
What am I excellent at?
What am I passionate about?
What am I not good at?
What am I terrible at?
What do I like?
What do I love?
What do I not like?
What do I despise?
What makes me feel horrible?
My epitaph will be . . .

Now, add the word *really* for most of the questions above, like what do I really like about myself? The purpose of this is to move away from the middle ground. I don't just want to know what you don't like, I want to know what you really don't like. Considering this, have you changed any of your answers?

Now let's consider the concept further and think about what you despise. Understanding that develops a greater self-awareness and helps determine what you need to do to move toward passion and away from what you despise, in terms of career choice.

Carefully re-read and consider your responses. Are any of them similar to each other? If so, begin to group them together. Revisit your answers and change any responses. As you go through this exercise, begin to consolidate the information into a few statements. For me, examples are "I despise numbers and accounting," and "I am passionate about helping people." Clear patterns and common themes will emerge and form the basis for new and exciting career choices that will fit with what you're passionate about. Once you have gone through this exercise, begin to research jobs that fit into these criteria, and you will no doubt find employment opportunities that help you do what you love to do.

Select Wisely

Selecting your field of study is also important. In too many cases, I see students graduating with postsecondary degrees that do very little for their careers. Unfortunately, educational institutions don't do a good job of disclosing or directing students toward data about job prospects within certain fields, some of which have limited employment opportunities.

Universities are offering degree programs in disciplines that have very few employment opportunities available after graduation, and that's relative to the number of graduates themselves. They will continue to offer such programs as long as students enroll in them. While I understand that everyone has a choice, I'm suggesting that students research job prospects *prior* to selecting their program. Being educated and unemployable in your field of study is rarely consistent with achieving your maximum potential.

One of the things to look for in an employer is how much they are willing to pay you in relation to your worth. You should be paid fairly and what you believe you are worth to your employer. I recall when Shaquille O'Neal, one of the greatest basketball players of all time, signed a seven-year, $120 million contract to play for the Los Angeles Lakers in 1996. I was watching an interview where a reporter asked Shaquille about the size of the contract. He replied that instead of questioning him, they should be asking the Los Angeles Lakers how much money they would make from his services. His implication was that they wouldn't have paid him that much money if it wasn't worth it to them. His presence increased fan attendance, gave them the chance to compete for championships, increased concession and jersey sales and gave them the ability to attract top free agents to the team. These were all important considerations by the owners and management of the team.

I have been very fortunate in my life to have worked for companies that offered excellent remuneration, career advancement and working conditions. In fact, I have never negotiated a salary with any of my employers, and while that may sound strange, when I think about it now, every time I accepted a position internally or with a new company, it was a promotion. I was happy for the opportunity and the new position was always accompanied by a salary increase. I never considered that I had any kind of leverage for salary negotiation. I was of course interested in the remuneration that each opportunity offered but money was never my primary driver. If that had been the case, I wouldn't have moved to the head office from the sales division at Standard Life as some of our salespeople, especially in the retail division, earned more than the president. I just wanted to advance. I believed that the more I progressed within the company, the more money I'd eventually make.

Because I had no prior experience in the roles whenever I was promoted, I always started on the lower end of the salary scale for each new position, but by the time I was promoted again, usually within three years, I was earning a mid-level scale salary. And then the cycle would begin again. As a point of interest, during my first year as president of Standard Life, my salary was 55 percent of my predecessor's, and I eventually caught up a few years later. Never one to negotiate, I thought that whatever I was being paid was generous enough, and if I continued to work hard, everything would fall into place.

If you believe that you're not being paid what you're worth, an open and authentic discussion with your employer is warranted. However, don't be the person who is always looking to negotiate salary and calculate bonus payments to the penny. If you're in a good environment that pays and treats you well, expend your energy into working hard and striving to be your best. The money will always follow.

The Third One Is the Charm

Sometimes, it takes a few jobs to finally land in the one that is ideally suited for you.

One of my favorite professors while attending York University was Mr. K. J. Radford. He taught a class called Decision Analysis. I can't say enough good things about him. He was one of those professors whose class you absolutely did not want to miss, and each assignment was done to the best of your ability because you didn't want to disappoint him. He was intelligent, empathetic, always accessible and a really good human being. He was a Multiplier Effect for me.

I recall being engaged in conversation with him and others one day after class. We were all pondering our futures and what would happen after graduation. He listened carefully as we spoke. I was intent on graduating and obtaining a well-paying job that would provide many opportunities for advancement, despite the job market being difficult at that time. I wouldn't settle for anything less! Admittedly, I was anxious because I didn't have a good grasp of how to handle a formal job search. All of my previous employment opportunities were the result of references from friends or family. Mr. Radford just shook his head. "Joseph, this is a very difficult market at the moment. You will probably not have a choice when you first graduate. Just apply to as many opportunities as you can. Get into a job, and take it from there. The decision for where you will work will be made for you. You will find that your first job is the one that anyone will give you. Your second one is more of your choosing and will be the one that helps you understand what is out there for you based on what you like and what you don't like. Your third one is the one that you will stay at." Professor Radford put me at ease and reassured me that everything would be fine. In retrospect, this is exactly what happened to me when I decided to enter the corporate world. Canada Life offered me my first job in a position I didn't even know existed, US Group Underwriter. I moved to Cigna when I knew I wanted to move into sales. I then moved to Standard Life when I wanted to work for a larger company that offered more opportunities for advancement, and I stayed there for twenty years.

Don't Be a Very Good Average

Most companies, of any size, will generally have an employee annual performance review of some kind. These companies have formal programs in place with individual assessments that are performed annually, with three- or six-month reviews in between. It usually involves a combination of a written assessment alongside a discussion with someone in a superior position. If conducted as intended, as an honest and frank discussion, these are very effective. Too often though, the discussions can revolve around what an employee has done well and not so well and what skills are needed for career development. The resulting plan is usually one that addresses any shortfalls. I believe that this is fundamentally flawed and will result in people being very good average employees.

If we strive to be good at everything, at best, we become very good on average, and then we're not excellent at anything at all.

Working on weaknesses usually results in becoming good, but rarely does it result in becoming great.

That's not a good strategy if you want to become your best self. Progressive companies encourage employee plans that take good foundational skills and develop them into excellent ones. Simultaneously, if required, employees should have a plan that develops their weaknesses just enough that they don't hamper them in performing their jobs. It's difficult to change poor into excellent when it comes to skill, but it is possible to progress to a level that is sufficient. Overall, employers want their employees to be excellent in the areas required to perform optimally in their role and just well enough in others.

You're responsible for the actions that help you become the best you can be. If your employer is not helpful in this way, create your own development plan.

Record Profits for Years

The insurance industry in Canada is dominated by few suppliers due to consolidation. This is similar to many other industries—telecommunications, energy and gas included. In 1986, my first year in the industry, there were well over twenty credible suppliers who customers could select for their insurance and investment products. The competition was fierce, and pricing pressure, technology investments and constant innovation were required for companies to stay in business. Every company strived to do everything well. Today, there are fewer than five major carriers along with some regional, smaller players.

When I was senior vice president of Group Life and Health at Standard Life, we were a midsize carrier, competing mainly with three very large companies. We couldn't compete with the strategy of being good everywhere because we didn't have the size and scale of our major competition, and this provided a pricing advantage for them. When it came to our strategy, I decided to specialize within each major line of business. We'd focus on being the premier long-term disability (LTD) carrier in Canada, and our life insurance, extended health and dental products, would be acceptable and average (good enough). However, we'd invest heavily in long-term disability (excellent). There is greater profit potential in LTD because of a direct correlation between money invested in disability prevention and helping people get back to work due to disability, and profitability. In essence, the more we invested in disability prevention and treatment, the fewer claims were incurred. That meant more profit, and so that's what we did, and we became very successful at it. This made us excellent somewhere and good enough everywhere else, and it enabled Standard Life to compete against larger companies. This was our Multiplier Effect for achieving sustainable success in a highly competitive market.

When I became president of Standard Life in 2005, our overall company strategy was to keep doing what we were doing well and invest in businesses that needed improvement. As an example, in the insurance retail division, we invested heavily in a product that had small-scale, individual life insurance. We were trying to be good in an area that we didn't consider a strength, nor would it ever be for us. It didn't work well, and we eventually abandoned the life insurance product altogether. Then it was time for a strategic shift.

During the next planning cycle, our strategy team selected a product within each line of business that we were excellent at, and then we enhanced our investment in those. Other products within each line of business were good enough to compete but would not be the drivers of our business. We were going to be excellent somewhere and good enough everywhere else. I'm happy to say we went on to achieve record profits for years thereafter.

Great Part-Time, Not so Much Full-Time

While still at school, I worked in a shoe store, and I loved it. It was a part-time position during school hours and full-time during the summer holidays. That job paid for my car expenses and my entertainment throughout university, and I got a 6 percent straight commission for every shoe, boot or handbag I sold. It made me realize that the company generated gross revenue of ninety-four dollars for each one-hundred-dollar sale that I made—a classic example of the harder I worked, the more money someone else made. There was no graded scale. No commission rates increasing over a certain threshold to reward exceptional performance. Consistently, I sold approximately three thousand dollars' worth of merchandise each week and was paid one hundred and eighty dollars for my efforts. The remuneration model was similar for their full-time employees, with the exception being, they were paid a nominal weekly flat amount plus 5 percent commission. Hours were long, and pay was less than spectacular, but this model worked very well for the company, and they continued to increase their number of stores. It worked well for me as a student, and it was an excellent job, but as a career, I knew it was not conducive to achieving the greatness I envisioned for myself.

Having said all of this, I believe that everyone should work in retail for at least one year in their youth, as it helps build character and good working habits like punctuality, responsibility, people skills, managing money and good grooming. However, I don't recommend it as a chosen field of work when you are beginning your career. You may get stuck in the retail industry and eventually be replaced by a younger and cheaper version of yourself. That's the reality of many jobs within the industry.

Our goal should be to work and be remunerated fairly and rewarded for it while bringing new ideas to help improve the organization.

Smaller Can Be Better

It can be beneficial to work for a small employer during the early days of your career, as resources and support are more limited than in larger companies. That usually means you're required to do more things for yourself, which results in you developing a greater and more in-depth knowledge of the business and industry. You, more than likely, will not have a strong branding presence in the market as a smaller player. You'll also need to work differently (usually harder) to achieve success if you're operating in a competitive environment and competing for business with peers representing a larger company. That was my experience.

My first sales position was in the insurance industry in 1988, with a company called Cigna. It was a very large company in the US, and it had a small presence in Canada. As mentioned earlier, we were competing against at least twenty other companies for business, and most of those had strong branding, more resources and more capital. Some, like Canada Life, had been in Canada since 1825 and were very well known in the industry. It was my job to convince brokers, the intermediaries for clients, that our company could handle anything that the larger carriers could. Without many support personnel, I had to put together my own proposals and marketing materials, a task other carriers could get head office to do. I remember one of the brokers asking me whether we produced automated quarterly experience reports, which are quarterly summaries of the premiums and claims activities for clients. These were used not only to monitor how the plan was performing but as a gauge for what the renewal rates could look like at premium renewal time, and most companies had systems to automatically produce these reports. "Of course we do!" I replied, but we did not! I was certainly not about to admit it, however, and that possibly cost me sales opportunities. After that, for this particular broker, I would manually add all of the premiums and claims for a client, put the data on an Excel spreadsheet and send it off on a quarterly basis. It was painful, but I learned all about the premium collection and claims reporting processes.

Work Harder

Our offices at Standard Life were located in the same building as the sales office that belonged to one of our main competitors, Canada Life, and as a result, I often encountered their salespeople and managers in the coffee shop in the building. Coincidently, I'd been an underwriter at Canada Life and realized that the harder I worked, the more money the salespeople made. That realization made me want to be in sales, and I also wanted to join their team, so I requested an interview. At that time, my sales experience was limited, and as such I was not successful, but it paved the way for me to join Cigna, and eventually, Standard Life. The lesson is, of course, that every setback is an opportunity for something new. Much later, when I was promoted to sales manager at Standard Life, my first two hires were salespeople from the Canada Life office as I knew them well, and it made sense to have them join my team.

One day, I bumped into Canada Life's manager in the coffee shop, and we were chatting about nothing in particular when the topic turned to salespeople. He mentioned that he wished he had the opportunity to send his salespeople to a smaller company for a year so they could learn how to sell more effectively. He thought that because their company was so large and well known to its customers, his salespeople didn't have to work as hard as they should for sales. He wondered how much the logo of Canada Life was responsible for their sales.

He obviously didn't know how good some of the members of his team were because the company offered a great deal of support.

So understand that if you work for a smaller employer, in a market that contains larger and better-known competitors, you need to work harder to succeed. Smaller employers often don't have the resources or the support that larger employers do, and this proved advantageous for me early in my career.

Full-Time Hobbies Can Be Life-Changing

Selecting a hobby that fuels your passion can have a profound effect on your ability to maximize your potential. These hobbies can range from martial arts training to dog grooming and everything in between. Engaging in an activity that you're passionate about will inevitably influence everything else that you do. As I'm a certified yoga instructor, I'll use this as a reference. Many yoga studios offer teacher training courses where interested students can enroll for a variety of reasons. Yogis in training will deepen their practice, increase their self-awareness and learn more about yoga culture from a two-hundred-hour program, which is the most commonly taught. It skims the surface of yoga and covers a variety of topics in brief detail. Some colleagues in my class joined to improve their self-esteem, while others wanted to teach yoga or open new studios themselves. Once a graduate of the training is accredited to teach yoga classes, they normally seek full- or part-time teaching opportunities. Personally, I enrolled to teach classes initially, and I began to do that soon after receiving my certificate. However, I realized that it was the spark that ignited my lifelong interest in learning how a spiritual awakening can harmoniously coexist with a materialistic view of life. I became captivated by the possibilities. My ongoing yogic learning has enhanced all things in my personal and business life and has led me to write this book.

We Like You, but You Need to Go

One day, while looking for a set of golf clubs at a local golf store in Montreal, I met a man named Mik. I was never an avid golfer, but

Jocelyn, the chair of our board, suggested that it would be a good way for me to interact with the Montreal business community as I'd be invited to many fundraising golf tournaments. Besides that, he wanted me to join his club, and he knew it would be a very good networking opportunity.

Mik was the salesman who took care of me at Golf Town, and I have to say, he was outstanding. I explained my situation to him by saying, "I'm a terrible golfer, and I've not played in years, so I need something that will be good enough to suit my purpose." Mik didn't oversell to me, nor did he try to sell me anything that I didn't need. As a matter of fact, what he offered was a set of golf clubs that were the previous year's model and said that if I enjoyed them, and the game, I could go back the following year, trade them in and upgrade as desired. That's how I got started again, and I began to enjoy it. After that, I was often in the store purchasing one thing or another, including a set of clubs for my wife and each of my children, and I always bought from Mik. If he wasn't working, I wasn't buying.

One day, I asked him what he was doing selling golf clubs in a retail store as I thought he was capable of so much more. He told me that soon he'd be graduating from McGill University and would be seeking employment opportunities. Then I explained that I worked for Standard Life and told him we were always looking for good people, so I asked for his resume and passed it along to our Senior Vice-Presidents (SVPs) of Human Resources and Finance, both of whom interviewed him. Mik was offered a position in Finance, and within six months, he was working on a very important document that was produced each month.

After about two years, Mik asked whether he could meet with me, and he told me he was happy in Finance and he knew that we believed he had good potential for growth, but for him, something was missing. He'd always thought about becoming a lawyer and wondered whether he'd missed his opportunity now that he had a very good full-time job in an organization that could offer increased career possibilities. He was asking for my advice, and as we talked, I asked him questions, trying to gauge how passionate he felt about law. Eventually, I asked his age, which was under thirty, and so I simply said, "Mik, as much as we like you, you need to go. Go to law school. If you don't do it now, you never will."

He left Standard Life, was accepted at Université de Montréal and is currently a happy and very successful lawyer. He met his wife at law school, and I even went to their wedding. I'm happy to say they now have a growing family. I consider myself very fortunate to have been Mik's Multiplier Effect.

Distinguish Yourself—for the Right Reason

Make a statement and be known for something. Drawing attention to yourself and being noticed for the right reasons can serve as Multiplier Effects for you. Strive to be known as the one who specializes in a certain task or is the go-to person for something, even if that something is not within the scope of your current responsibilities.

Volunteering for projects in the workforce is a simple and effective way to make yourself more visible within the organization. This work is sometimes performed within a team outside of your department. The exposure to different people and the relationships that you develop will be useful later. You have an opportunity to demonstrate your skills and learn new ones. Successful projects are often presented to senior management, which can give you another opportunity to gain visibility within the company.

Being known at work doesn't just mean within senior management. Being known among all staff is important. Volunteering for company events and fundraisers and having lunch or coffee in the company cafeteria are ways to meet colleagues from other departments.

This principle also applies outside of the workplace. Have you noticed that there is always a go-to person that family and friends rely on for guidance? This could be tax advice, wardrobe choice for an important event or even the purchase of a new electronic device. There always seems to be a person who everyone naturally gravitates toward when they need help. Why do you think that happens? Probably because that person has helped many in the past and is viewed as an expert of sorts. I'd suggest that they have also made it known, through actions or words, that they are willing to help when asked. If you are this person, excellent. If not, strive to be.

Nice Things for People

Whenever someone was promoted or hired at Standard Life, Human Resources announced the news via our intranet. In my early years, that person was most often unknown to me. It didn't stop me from looking up their email address on the company directory and sending them a welcoming and congratulatory note. I thought that was a nice thing to do for a new or newly promoted person. I did this for many years.

One day, as a newly appointed SVP, I asked all of our VPs to arrange a tour of their departments so that I could meet their teams. During one visit to Customer Services, I stopped to speak to a manager at her cubicle. We chatted for a while, and as we were doing so, she pointed to a piece of paper pinned to her wall and said, "Remember this?" I looked closer, and there was a copy of the congratulatory note I had sent her when she'd been promoted years earlier. She told me that she thought it was very nice to receive a note from someone she'd never even met. People will remember nice things that you do for them, no matter how great or small.

Days, weeks, years, we don't remember.
Special moments, we always remember.

A simple way to distinguish yourself is through your wardrobe and personal grooming habits. Whether we agree or not, people notice how we look and our fashion flair. If you look good, you feel good, so dress like the person you want to be. This should apply in both your work and personal life. At work, I always dressed for my next role, always wearing a suit, fashionable shirt, tie, polished shoes, a nice watch, and well-groomed nails. Early in my career, I wore white shirts. They provided a blank slate that meant I could wear any tie and not try to match it to my shirt. I was known for having a great selection of ties. Here is an important piece of advice that many have learned the hard way—never wear shirts that show perspiration stains. NEVER!

Casual dress days at work provide an opportunity to distinguish yourself. Business casual is more than jeans and a blazer. Actually, I've never worn jeans at the workplace. I just think that they're too casual. Trust me, people notice if you dress well. Develop a personal dress code that works for you as a simple and effective way to distinguish yourself. If you work in an environment that is casual dress every day, use this as a baseline and dress it up a little.

The Diminishing Effect of Presentation

I've often heard and agree with the idea of dressing for success. Being stylish while adding a little bit of tasteful individuality just makes sense to me. However, have you ever come across, as I have on numerous occasions in my career, those who went too far in the other direction of trying to be stylish and found themselves outside of the company dress code or industry culture? While individuality is important, sometimes too much individuality can make you seem as if you're not as much a part of the team and can have a diminishing Multiplier Effect.

Dressing appropriately for your current and future roles will have a Multiplier Effect on your career. Even in a world that is more sensitive to such issues and is more politically correct, it's a fact. Not considering the importance of this reality and adjusting accordingly will have a Diminishing Effect on your life and career.

Finding your ideal occupation will have a profound effect on maximizing your potential, however, we cannot discover the opportunities that are available until we discover our true selves. A part of our self-discovery is spiritual, of course, as we discussed in Chapter 3. Another part is more practical, in the sense that we need to understand who we are and what we are passionate about to find a career that we can thrive in. We began this portion of our journey with the What is Your ideal Job questionnaire in this chapter. For most of us, a career has a shelf life, and we eventually retire. We owe it to ourselves to look for work that brings out the best in us. Briefly reflect on what the Multiplier Effects are in this chapter and select which ones will help bring out the best in you:

- Selecting your ideal career
- Don't be just average
- Work harder than the rest
- Distinguish yourself

Are you in your ideal career? If not, what are you going to do about it?

CHAPTER 7

Never Stop Learning

Our brains have an unlimited capacity for storing information. Does it not make sense therefore to learn as much as you can for as long as you can?

What you retain as you gather information from books, teachers, podcasts, social media, television and wherever else is a beginning. It's preparing you to learn. Memorizing information is an excellent start—but it's just part of the learning process.

True learning is achieved through experiencing something.

Imagine reading an article or watching a documentary about the Amazon Jungle. You may be able to say that you learned a great deal and now know something you didn't know before. But through that, you learned what someone else wrote or filmed, and it's their interpretation of it. It's how they chose to present it. Ask yourself, "What have I really learned?" If you visit the jungle yourself, you'll be part of it. You can live it, experience it and thus truly learn about it.

The humble one is the one who will experience the greatest learning.

Humble Enough to Learn

Understand that it's perfectly acceptable to not be fully prepared for any particular task or situation. This should motivate you to learn as much as possible for what needs to be done, but you cannot be 100 percent prepared for anything, let alone everything. I'm certainly never fully prepared.

In my experience with relatively senior roles that carry responsibility within the corporate environment, it takes about three years to be completely comfortable in a role that's new to you. As I mentioned earlier, I was fortunate to have been promoted more or less every three years at Standard Life. Coincidentally, just as I became comfortable with every aspect of my new role, a new challenge presented itself. Surrounding myself with a good team I could trust was paramount in overcoming not being properly prepared, and it allowed me time to grow my competency in that new role.

As president, I never felt fully prepared for any presentation or meeting I conducted or attended. There was never enough time to read through all of the material, practice in front of a podium or memorize the key points. It caused me a great deal of stress at first, but after a while, I realized it would be virtually impossible to do, given the volume of meetings, commitments and material that required reviewing on a daily basis. The solution was simple—be as prepared as possible and surround myself with experts in topics that I was not well-versed in. As an example, during meetings with external auditors, I'd prepare as best as I could, but knowing that intricate financial reporting was a challenge, Christian, our chief financial officer, would always be invited for support. Between the two of us, we were able to cover everything required for our meeting. The learning process sometimes means understanding that someone else will always know more than you do and that you should outsource your learning to them.

My First Board Meeting

When my first board meeting with our Canadian board members was coming up, I read and re-read the package of information sent to the board members several days in advance and carefully looked at the agenda. This was to determine where my participation would be required, and I studied the material as if I were writing an important exam. Our board members were all seasoned executives with plenty of experience, and they'd achieved much success. This was rather intimidating. I didn't want to embarrass myself, my team members attending the meeting or our group chief executive, who'd recently appointed me to the role. A few moments before the meeting, as everyone was entering the boardroom, I was standing in the doorway, letting everyone in before me. Sandy must have sensed my nervousness as he took me aside and counseled me to just be a leader. That simple advice calmed me down.

Our experts led most of the presentations and discussions within their areas of expertise, and I handled any questions and provided commentary as required. My primary responsibility was to help orchestrate the agenda, and with the support of all attendees, the meeting was a success. My nervousness subsided, and the experience gave me a sense of ease for future meetings.

Something similar happened when I attended my first meeting with the Canadian Council of Chief Executives. The council was composed of CEOs and entrepreneurs from approximately one hundred and fifty leading Canadian companies. Those meetings lasted all day. The heavyweights in Canadian business were all members, and then there was me, Joseph. Being in a room with these executives was intimidating—most were household names within the business community. Besides saying hello, I barely spoke to anyone. Instead, I listened carefully to all of the speakers and presentations and took copious amounts of notes, but during a break, everything changed. Everyone was cordial, friendly and welcoming, but my attitude and insecurity was getting in the way of me being my best self. A change was necessary. Subsequent meetings were different as I networked aggressively, making a point to speak to many leaders and learn as much as possible from them. One can never have too many contacts.

By constantly reminding myself of my strengths and reverting back to one of the things that made me successful—my ability to interact with people—I became comfortable outside of my comfort zone, and in this case, that is a Multiplier Effect for me.

Speaking of comfort zones, I will always encourage you to live beyond yours. That's the only way you can expand your physical and mental horizons to be your best possible self. Reverting to your strengths while outside of your comfort zone will put you at ease and calm any anxiety you may have. Let's consider an example. As mentioned earlier, financial statement literacy is not a strength of mine, so contributing positively in a financially technical discussion is a challenge. Therefore, instead of being uncomfortable, I guide the conversation back to my strengths, usually relating the numbers back to something familiar. If a discussion is taking place regarding the financials of a company, I don't try to determine how the numbers are calculated. This is counterproductive and not one of my strengths. I determine how the numbers could affect the performance of the company and how they'll impact the execution of our strategy. This enables me to contribute positively to the discussion by focusing on my area of expertise, strategic acumen.

Know When You Know Enough

*When the learning stops,
the exit begins.*

Once you have stopped learning from a person or a situation, it's time to take that learning and apply it somewhere else as you continue your journey to maximum potential. I played a lot of sports in my youth and always made it a point to play with kids that were older and better than I was. Early on, more games and battles were lost than won, but eventually, I ended up being more proficient than most. When there was little left to learn, I moved on. This was part of my learning and experience.

A good example is my tennis journey. I enjoyed the game of tennis as a teenager and wanted to be the best player I could be. My family didn't have the money for me to join a tennis club, so we played daily at the local asphalt courts during summers. Many of us just showed up at the courts and played whoever was available, and there, I purposely played older kids, who were stronger, had a better serve and could hit the ball harder and more accurately than me. They didn't mind because, early on, it was an easy victory for them. Eventually, I began to improve my game, studied their weaknesses and was more competitive. My formal coaching was from a tennis book, purchased for twenty-five cents at the local supermarket. It's still a prized possession in my bookcase. Once the learning and improvement began to slow down and winning became easier, I figured I'd learned enough and moved on to play others, always looking for players who I could learn something from—a left-hander whose spin on the ball was different than I was used to, or someone who was especially adept at serving and so on. This is how I improved my game and became a very competitive player.

This principle will always apply while you're striving to become your best self. Always select friends, partners, employers and jobs that you can learn a great deal from. These are the ones that you will maintain long relationships with. Partners and friends that stay for a long time are the ones who constantly help you learn new things, quite often by sharing new things that they've learned.

Visualize, Visualize, Visualize

Visualization is important in the learning process because it sets the stage for true learning.

The concept of visualization has been important in my life for as long as I can remember. My parents worked separate shift work until I was eight years old, and it was rare that both of them were home at the same time during this period. There was not much to do after school, and television programs for kids were limited to a couple of shows during the late afternoon. Some of my time after dinner was spent reading or playing with toys, and I'd often play chess against myself. Maybe it's the Libra in me, but winning and losing to myself in the same game was acceptable because there was a sense of balance in the result. Oftentimes, I'd lie on the floor, close my eyes and visualize myself playing professional hockey or being the lead singer of a band playing to a sold-out audience. In retrospect, having an active imagination was a pleasant by-product of being an only child in a time where entertainment, at least within the home, was limited.

Visualization helps determine which strategies might work. When I played sports, I'd often visualize how plays could unfold during the game. This helped me prepare should a similar situation arise during a play. I usually played center field in baseball. With each opponent player in the batter's box, I visualized where they could potentially hit the ball, what my reaction would be and to which teammate the ball should be thrown. I'd visualize as many scenarios as possible in between pitches and batters. Many times, especially if I knew a hitter's tendencies, one of my visualization scenarios would play out in real life.

To this day, I still use visualization as an important tool to help me perform to the best of my abilities in any given situation. The usefulness is obvious while preparing for a situation that's important, like a speech, a presentation or even a wedding ceremony. I also find visualization to be effective in everyday activities, such as performing household chores or shopping. If I decide to paint a room, for example, I'll envision which wall to begin with, where to place the furniture, and which areas might present problems. This helps me prepare for performing the task at an optimal level.

As an avid people watcher, I especially love to watch people I admire or can learn from. Watching what they do, how they do it, how they move, and listening to what they say helps me visualize doing it myself. I learned many new skills from something simple like throwing a football or swinging a golf club to something a little more complicated like giving a speech just by watching people. Use visualization as a training manual.

I also used to visualize what my next job would be. As a manager, I visualized being a VP and imagined strategies I'd employ. I worked on who would be my key team members and how to implement new initiatives, and I always visualized what was coming next. Now I realize that this is a technique used by people who understand the

Law of Attraction, which I explained briefly in Chapter Two. This is about using the power of your mind to manifest your thoughts into reality. Everything begins as a thought, and with enough focus, your thoughts can materialize into something real. I'm convinced that the use of visualization throughout my life has helped me in my journey to becoming my best self.

Everyone's Story Is Fascinating

Along with my extensive airplane travels, I've also taken many cab rides in various cities and always make it a practice to strike up a conversation with the driver. Curious about them as a person, I ask about their birthplace, cultural background, what was beautiful about their home country, why they're driving a specific car and whether they have a family. There is much to learn from striking up a conversation with a stranger. I also often wonder how they came to be a taxi driver. The stories are very interesting.

A cabbie in Montreal, from Lebanon, explained how his family owned and operated a luggage factory, but due to political instability and turmoil in the country, they left everything behind and immigrated to Canada. I learned how the company designed luggage, what materials were used and how they distributed their products. Another driver was a physician from Central African Republic. It's French-speaking, and they've had turmoil since 2012 and their health system is barely functioning. He couldn't practice in Canada and was studying to obtain proper credentials, driving a cab in the meantime to earn a living. I learned how difficult it can be to attain Canadian equivalent medical credentials for foreign medical doctors. People are the most interesting creatures, and everyone has a story that we can learn from.

Seeing Double

Sometimes, I'll mentally clone myself, then imagine leaving my body to observe what's happening. Then I ask myself, "Are you happy and satisfied with what you see?"

It allows me to imagine how others see me in that particular situation. There is always opportunity for improvement. I ask myself what I can do to make sure that I'm not only doing my best, but that I'm also being perceived as doing my best by others. This is important. Giving 100 percent effort in everything you do helps you achieve your maximum potential, but it's equally important that everyone knows you're giving that 100 percent by the results of your words and actions. We have a natural attraction to and an admiration for people who are always striving to be their best.

As an example, when in front of an audience giving a speech or presentation, I scan the crowd and isolate a few participants from different angles. Even though I may not know them, they'll be my visual points of reference throughout the presentation. I imagine myself sitting in their seat with me in their line of sight. What do they see? Do I look confident? Are there any distractions? Does my body language match my verbal presentation? If something doesn't seem right from their perspective, I make adjustments to ensure the experience is optimum for everyone in attendance.

The First Time Makes So Many Things Better

Your first experience with something serves as a Multiplier Effect for learning. You will learn a great deal from a first experience. A multi-Multiplier Effect happens when you take your first experience with something and apply it to other scenarios.

An example: during my first public speech, I was extremely nervous and mostly looked down to read from my document. This gave the (correct) impression that I was reading, as opposed to speaking, to the audience. The feedback from my colleagues was not favorable. They reminded me that one of my strengths was speaking from the heart with emotion, something that couldn't be done by reading words on a page. I needed to live and feel the words and express them in a manner that was uniquely mine. Understanding this, I handled the preparation for my next speaking engagement differently. I practiced it more so I could I recite most of it verbatim with an occasional glance at the written text and so I could stray from the script on occasion. I delivered that speech much more effectively and with my unique flair, and it was received significantly better than my first.

What I learned from this experience helped me with many other undertakings. I was able to conduct more effective presentations while participating in board and employee meetings. That experience also helped me explain and articulate ideas more efficiently in any group setting. The first learning was a multi-Multiplier Effect—taking the experience from my first speech and applying it to different scenarios. Can you think of a Multiplier Effect that effectively became a multi-Multiplier Effect for you?

The learning process is complicated, and mostly, it begins with memory retention, an important step. But as I mentioned earlier, true learning comes only with experience. That's because all our senses are in play when we experience something, and it's down to this that we have an active recall mechanism for retaining and retrieving the information gathered from that experience.

Let's illustrate this with an example The concept is similar to the one mentioned earlier regarding the Amazon Jungle, but more practical. Imagine walking along a path on a trail or forest close to your home. There are many trees, and some are so tall that they seem to touch the sky. Others are tiny and struggle to find room to grow. Imagine them as vividly as you can. The taller trees have rough bark. Reach out to touch them. What does it feel like? All kinds of leaves are swaying gently on their branches as a soft breeze whistles gently through the air. Can you hear it? The ground beneath your feet is an uneven mixture of soil, rocks, fallen branches and small plants. At times, the air feels clear and fresh, and at others, it's heavy and humid as you continue along your path. What do you smell? What do you hear? Little creatures, insects and birds are abundant, some of which you can see and others you can only hear, and you wonder what they're up to. Through this exercise, you have learned what it's like to walk through this particular forest.

Now, what would your learning about the forest be if you actually experienced walking through it with the same keen awareness and curiosity as you experienced visualizing walking on the path? Certainly, your senses would be activated. You'd have felt the soft breeze on your face and the rough bark on the tall trees. You'd have experienced the smells of the forest and heard the branches tapping against each other. You'd have felt the uneven ground underfoot and seen how small the trees were. And you'd have seen some of those creatures you were listening to. It would be an authentic experience of walking through the forest, and by doing this exercise, you would not just have learned about that forest but you would have experienced it. This is true learning.

Close your eyes and take this moment to visualize yourself as someone who has an insatiable appetite for learning and is always focused on developing their strengths. Watch yourself from above as you stride through life with the confidence of someone who knows who they are and what they want. How does that feel?

CHAPTER 8

Decisions, Decisions

Find the Funny.

I encourage you to always find happiness within your surroundings and to strive to be in a state of joyfulness. You'll make your best decisions in this state.

We discussed this in detail in Chapter 3. If you're unhappy, try to catch it so that you can do something about that and shift state. Think of something funny, play music, watch a video or just look up at the sky. Whatever works for you is fine. When looking for something that will make me happy, I observe what's around me and play a game called "Find the Funny."

If we look carefully, humor is everywhere, and it's usually related to people. People are always doing funny things. Observe a facial expression of a parent giving their child a driving lesson or how someone selects their vegetables at the supermarket, and you'll understand what I mean. Whoever or whatever you're watching, do nothing other than observe. No judgments, just watch. You'll find funny. Sometimes, I look in the mirror, remember a funny incident or joke and break out laughing all by myself.

Finding funny in pets is easy too. Watching one of my dogs, Frankie or Leo, attempting to bury a treat in our sofa never gets tiring. Playing this game takes me back to childhood, when happiness was found everywhere. Being in a happy state of mind is important for making decisions that are best for you because your best decisions will be made when you're joyful and happy. Most importantly, avoid anger as much as possible. If you do become angry, try not to let it linger and absolutely avoid making any decisions when you're in that state. Anger leads to compulsiveness, which rarely allows you to make the best decision.

Think about how you act when you're happy. Do you feel energized, enthusiastic, motivated and more open to new ideas? Most people do. Now, think about how you act when you're angry. Are you quick to react without taking the time to think and more likely to make emotional judgments and decisions? That's the norm. People are their most irrational selves when they're angry. Think about how many times you've immediately regretted doing something because you did it when you were angry—road rage, buyer's remorse and verbal abuse are some examples of anger leading to poor, regrettable decisions.

It can be trying at times, but striving to be in a constant state of happiness and joyfulness will ensure that, most often, you'll make the right decisions, given the circumstances and information available to you at that time.

There is no better time than now to let go of what does not serve you. You are postponing the inevitable. And it will be more painful.

Understanding Our Decision-Making Process

On average, we make thousands of decisions per day. Most of them are unconscious, but the ones that are most important are the conscious ones.

The basis for decision-making is essentially the same for everyone. Firstly, we take what facts are available to us, which can involve research or assessment of what's presented to us as salient information related to the decision. Secondly, we mine our memory for a similar experience. This is important, as we determine what we've learned through our senses in past experiences and then use this to guide us. Thirdly, we consider what we have learned from our education as it relates to a particular decision. The current circumstances and the environment is our next consideration, and finally, we rely on intuition, which oftentimes is a deciding factor. Emotion factors in as well sometimes.

These are the fundamental elements of our decision-making process, and each of us assigns a percentage of importance to each element, based on who we are as individuals. Depending on the type of person you are, each percentage is weighted differently. Someone who is more inclined toward mathematical and linear thinking will have a greater weighting in the factual elements, while someone who is more liberal thinking or entrepreneurial will more likely have a heavier weighting on intuition. Having self-awareness and understanding the type of individual you are will, inevitably, guide how you make and influence good decisions.

Understanding other parties will help influence their decisions. If you want to convince someone of something or change their mind, have a good understanding of who they are as an individual. This will help you recognize their decision-making process. As an example, when speaking to an accountant in a work situation, I can determine what they'll need to make or confirm a decision. Being mathematically inclined, they reason with facts, charts, historical data and formulas. The information must be clear, logical, as comprehensive as possible, and most importantly, confirmed as accurate because they know the laws, rules and regulations that govern their profession. I estimate that these elements weigh heavily for this type of individual to come to a conclusion or commitment, and I prepare as such. Knowing this and being properly prepared is essential to any conversation in business or otherwise. Salespeople, in contrast, don't seem to need as much data. They're naturally entrepreneurial, have a healthy risk tolerance and place greater emphasis on intuition than most. There's a reason that most good salespeople live by the saying, "It's easier to ask forgiveness than to get permission."

I have two core ways of making decisions, and they have served me well throughout my career and personal life. They are called 1) "Kill or Cure" and 2) "Appropriate for Now."

1) Kill or Cure

Whenever I'm confronted with a decision or a situation that needs to be dealt with, I immediately decide whether to kill it or cure it. There's no good in postponing the inevitable. It's either resolved, or it's time to move on. If a situation can be resolved, then develop a plan to cure it. If a situation can't be resolved, kill it immediately and move on. There are too many other things to do that require your attention than to waste your time procrastinating. As an example, if someone at work is a problem and is negatively affecting you or your company, immediately deal with that situation in a positive manner (cure) or terminate/change the relationship (kill). A healthy and productive conversation can be a cure or can result in the realization that you can't work with this person in a productive manner. Never let the problem linger or go unattended because it'll affect your ability to be your best self. It's also unfair to everyone involved, and you're simply delaying what will happen anyway. Here's a real-life example that happened to me several times in my career. Because I was fortunate enough to have been promoted internally for most of my career, I ended up being the boss of my former colleagues whenever this happened. On some occasions, not everyone supported my promotion. I did my best to show them that I appreciated their help and support as we continued to work together, and for the most part, it worked out well. However, sometimes there was someone that I just could not win over for their support. In such cases, I encouraged them to look for opportunities outside of our team. The principle applies in any professional or personal situation. If you're in a relationship that has become strained or has somehow changed negatively, kill it or cure it. Suppressing resentment and avoiding the issues that caused the strain is not a good strategy. Avoid outsourcing the cure to something else unless it's professional therapy. I've known couples who decided that having a child would somehow miraculously resolve their marital issues. It did not. Immediately, a discussion must be had and a plan must be made to move forward in a manner that returns the relationship to a healthy state, and if this isn't possible, then the relationship needs to change or end. Making such a decision is certainly difficult, especially when there's a deep emotional attachment, and summoning the courage and resolve can be daunting, but in the long term, it's important and always works best for everyone. If too many things are left lingering with no resolution in sight, too much energy will be spent on things that take away from being your best self. Healthy personal relationships, which will be discussed in greater length in a later chapter, are a catalyst to achieving your maximum potential.

Always address any situation directly and don't procrastinate. There are too many things happening simultaneously in your life, and new ones are being added daily. Excess clutter within your mind will make it more difficult to make correct decisions with clarity.

2) Appropriate for Now

The principle of Appropriate for Now is understanding the right thing to do or say *right* at this moment. It's of great importance when dealing with a situation on a timely basis. It sometimes naturally follows the principle of Kill or Cure. The initial decision is how to tackle the situation head-on, hence Kill or Cure. The next decision is what's the most advantageous and effective action to take *at that time*. In other words, what's Appropriate for Now? However, we can't just deal with it irrationally for the sole purpose of resolving an issue. We must determine the appropriate thing to do while we consider a resolution.

I recommend always considering what's Appropriate for Now, and this can be in the form of actions or words. Appropriate for Now doesn't have time considerations as it can last for two minutes, two months or two years—the length of time doesn't matter. It means doing what's right in the present moment, given the situation and information at hand. All you need to do is ask yourself, "What's appropriate for now?" Can you think of something that applies to you right now? What's the appropriate thing to do at this moment? Are you doing it? Doing what's appropriate at all times will ensure that you live in the moment while considering past and future circumstances and the consequences of your decision.

Let's consider a couple of examples. Let's say you're questioning your current career choice. The Appropriate for Now career choice that you made years ago may be no longer valid, and a new one might be needed. Once you've made your Kill or Cure decision (in this case Kill), and you have decided to make a change, a series of Appropriate for Now decisions are followed by subsequent decisions:

- What will be my new career choice? (What's appropriate for me at this time in my life?)

- What will be required of me? Going back to school? (What's the appropriate school?)
- Do I need to learn a new skill? (What's the appropriate skill?)
- Do I have adequate financial resources? (What's the appropriate method of securing them?)
- What are the implications for my family? Will there be a disruption of the current family dynamic that will require additional help or support from others? (What's the appropriate way to deal with this?)

These are decisions that will need to be made in order to make the career change successful.

Let's take another example. You're invited to a formal dinner by your company where you'll meet the senior management for the first time. There are many Appropriate for Now decisions to be made in this scenario. The choice of attire is a significant one. Proper table etiquette may be another. How will you interact with your colleagues? How much should you drink at the event? These are important Appropriate for Now decisions that can affect how others perceive you and possibly influence your career.

Making the right decisions that are appropriate for the circumstances should always be what's appropriate for you. Most importantly, never compromise your beliefs, integrity or values when considering what to say or do at any given time.

The Spiritual Aspect of Decision Making

The pineal gland located in your brain is referred to as the Third Eye. Awakening it can bring about spiritual growth and increased intuition. If you recall, earlier in this chapter, we discussed the various elements involved in the decision-making process, one of which was intuition. Intuition can weigh differently for each person during decision-making, but it's a very important element for some. We all know people who make important decisions based on their "gut feelings." Therefore, if you can increase your intuition through the awakening of the Third Eye, it stands to reason that your decision-making ability will benefit from that. We are three-dimensional beings living in a three-dimensional world and see things as such. Opening our Third Eye helps us to see things beyond our normal vision. This is extremely useful when tapping into greater knowledge sources that help us view things with greater clarity. An open Third Eye can elevate your perception of all things.

Many of us use our senses, especially our eyes and ears, to confirm what we perceive as being the truth. We want to see the proof. We need to hear it for ourselves. Everyone has heard the phrase, "See it to believe it." This is a perfectly understandable and useful approach, and it can serve us well. However, based on the state of the world we live in, we can't rely on just our senses to determine the truth. Today, the world is full of people and organizations that blend facts with fake news as part of the "truthful information" that is available to us. Propaganda is everywhere. Artificial intelligence has advanced to a point where we can develop any story we wish by manipulating a video and claiming it's the truth for instance. It looks and sounds real, but it's not, and because of this, it can lead to poor decision-making. We are no longer just being bombarded by information from many different mediums, we are, more than ever, confronted with an avalanche of factual information and misinformation. We can no longer just sift through the information and decide what's relevant at any point in time. Instead, we now need to determine what's truthful first. This phenomenon leads to information fatigue, and more importantly, distraction, and it's important to remember that we don't make good decisions when we're distracted.

That's why it's imperative to approach each situation with an open mind and rely on more than just our senses. We can't assume that our senses, especially our eyes and ears, will be honest with us because what they see and hear contains more untruths than ever.

Since opening my Third Eye, things have become a lot clearer. I've always considered myself someone who can quickly cut through the clutter and get to the heart of an issue immediately and thus make good decisions quickly. My intuition is almost always right. I can envision how things unfold easily, and I can now see with greater depth and richness what is around me beyond the obvious. Connecting the dots is easier and comes quicker than before, and I'm convinced that had I realized how important opening my Third Eye was early in my career, I'd have been successful faster and would have made better decisions in my personal life. Can you imagine the impact of having enhanced intuition in a working environment, as an entrepreneur for example? Especially in a world that's changing almost by the minute.

As I've continued to work on opening my Third Eye, I have a greater sense of who I am as a human being, and I understand more clearly my purpose within our universe. Throughout my corporate career, I defined myself and believed that others would define me by what was accomplished at work. High levels of achievement and the materialistic rewards that accompanied it were paramount in my thinking. I was very competitive and envious of others' achievements and successes, which was measured by the accumulation of material things. More was better, and more of everything was better still.

Currently, I still like to have nice things and believe that if you work hard and honestly for something, you deserve to reward yourself and others, if that's your desire. There's nothing wrong with that, but the difference in my thinking today is that I don't want more than I need, although I'm still working on that.

As a youth, I recall my dad saying, "You know you've made it when you can afford a Cadillac." In those days, owning a Cadillac was the pinnacle of success and achievement. Unfortunately, my dad passed away in 1988 and wasn't here to see that I achieved what he'd desired for me when he arrived from Italy all those years ago. I'd always said that, at some point in my life, I needed to own a Cadillac to show my dad that I'd made it. Now, I'm not so sure. Maybe a toy model for my desk will be just fine.

Opening the Third Eye is not a difficult process, but it does involve commitment and discipline. There are many sources of information available that will help you, and I encourage you to do some research and find what's best suited for you.

If you have a question, look no further than the universe and its infinite wisdom. It always responds. Understanding its form of communication is key.

Look for Signs

Sometimes I meditate and ask the universe for guidance, especially when I need to make an important decision. Asking for a sign helps me decide what the right course of action is in any given situation. Sometimes, I'll just float an idea out there and be patient, knowing that some kind of sign will present itself and help guide me. The responses, for me at least, usually come in the form of numbers. Specifically, the number six.

My very first interview for the President and CEO of Standard Life position was scheduled on October 6, 2004—my birthday. October 6, the tenth month and the sixth day—one hundred and six. The year 2004—2+0+0+4=6. Coincidence? I don't think so. The interview went very well.

The numbers 6, 106, 610 and 1061 have followed me around for my entire life, and they have always been associated with good things. This is especially true with the number 6. My birthdate is October 6 (106) 1961. My life number is 6. Because these numbers show up ALL the time, I know the universe, a spirit guide or guardian angel is letting me know that I'm in the right place or have made the right decision.

Is there something that keeps appearing in your life at specific times? A number? A color? Something else? If nothing comes to mind immediately, think carefully. There is usually something. Then, pay attention when it appears. It's a sign. I also encourage you to calculate your life number and notice whether it keeps appearing in your life.

Don't Forget to Ask

Once you've decided what you want, ask for it. How many times have you been disappointed at not obtaining something you desire? Did you ask?

Don't assume everyone can read your mind. You may give hints about what you want, believing you're crystal clear in your intention, only to discover that no one quite understood what you meant. How often have you heard or even asked yourself, "Why was I not asked?" Or "Why didn't I get considered?" Was the response, "I didn't know you were interested?" These are missed opportunities, so always make your intentions known, and when asking for something, be clear and concise so there can be no misunderstanding. That way not only is there an opportunity to obtain what you want, but the clarity of your intent will signal to others to keep you top of mind for opportunities. Assuming you have the credentials, you'll be a natural choice to be considered or even given an opportunity when one arises. Clear intentions are appreciated.

Knowing who to ask and understanding who the decision-maker is or who is influential in the decision-making will be critical in obtaining what you desire. Sometimes, it'll be as obvious as the title of a person in the corporate environment or a respected family member. At others, you'll need to determine who has the power to say yes to you.

Often, people will have the power or influence to say no but not have the power to say yes. Don't ignore these individuals as they are just as important as people with the ability to say yes to an opportunity.

Let's consider an example. At Standard Life, if we were fortunate enough to be considered as a finalist for obtaining an account, we'd be asked, with the other finalist companies, to make a sales pitch presentation to our prospective customer. Usually, the main influencers in the client's decision-making process were representatives from finance and human resources. Finance's role is to secure the best possible price, while human resources' role is to secure the best possible plan for employees. The administrator, usually within human resources, deals with the administration of the plan on a day-to-day basis. Too often, the administrator's role is minimized during the pitch presentations because the sales teams focus on the primary decision-makers. However, ignoring the administrator is foolish, and it can be detrimental. This person can't say yes to you, but they can say no. If our plan offered the best price and a competitive package but was difficult to administer, we'd hamper our opportunity to obtain the business because the administrator believed that their job would be more difficult. If the administrator determined that our offer would make their job easier and more efficient, they'd positively influence the decision. They're powerful influencers and shouldn't be discounted in any way. We coached our teams to always consider the administrator during sales pitches because, quite often, they had the informal power to influence the final decision.

No-Regret Decisions

We always want to make decisions that we will not regret. We make so many decisions per day, it would be impossible to question whether each one is a no-regret one. However, we can do this for most decisions that we make consciously.

When making a decision, get into the habit of asking yourself whether you could live with that same decision on the day you make it, the following week, the following month and the following year. Sometimes, the timeline won't apply, and the decision will be of little importance, like what shoes you should wear to yoga class, but start asking yourself the question, nonetheless. If it's the right thing to do, at that particular time, given the information available and circumstances (remember Appropriate for Now), go for it. It may be a decision that doesn't work out as planned, but if it was appropriate at the time it was made, that's fine, and you shouldn't regret it. This applies to any decision you make, and by asking yourself the question, you'll also encourage yourself to gather the right amount of information as part of that process.

We make thousands of decisions every day. Usually, decisions lead to other decisions that need to be made. That's how the world works. The ability to make good decisions consistently is dependent on your decision-making process, and it'll help you be at your best always.

Let's summarize some of the Multiplier Effects in this chapter that will help you make good decisions:

- Happy people make better decisions
- Never let something linger—Kill it or Cure it
- Always do what is Appropriate for Now
- Open your Third Eye
- The universe is speaking to you—look for the signs
- Don't be shy, ask for what you want
- You will never regret making a good decision

A sound decision-making process that is bespoke to you is crucial to your success, and it'll ultimately contribute to becoming your best self.

CHAPTER 9

The Team

Complementary Skill Set

As mentioned in an earlier chapter, one of my first jobs during university was selling shoes, and I was paid a commission based on sales. Working for two nights per week and Saturdays, while attending university, my weekly goal was to sell three thousand dollars' worth of shoes while being paid a 6 percent commission for all sales. This would result in $180, and that was mostly spent on gas and entertainment. One day, I asked my manager if I could change one of my nights from Tuesday to Wednesday. "Absolutely not!" he responded. "This will upset the balance of the store on those days." I asked for an explanation, and he stated that it was quite simple, and as an economics student looking for a career in a corporate environment, he was surprised I would need to ask. "It's how I set up the teams for each day of the week," he said.

He had a system for setting up his staff each day. He needed one "gunner," someone who could sell anything to anyone; one person who was good on displays, so that the store was kept clean; one person who could work the cash register in a pinch, if the store got busy; and finally, a person who didn't mind stocking shelves when new merchandise arrived. There were different types of salespeople on staff, and he played each to their individual strengths so that he had a strong, balanced team at all times during store hours. This resulted in a maximum opportunity for success. The teams were set with the sole goal of surpassing the day's sales targets and maintaining an efficiently run store. Too many gunners on the sales floor meant they would be overly competitive with each other, place more emphasis on sales and less on service, thus compromising the customer experience. On Tuesday and Friday nights, I was the gunner. The teams were set. Case closed and no more discussion.

In my manager's eyes, a complementary skill set in the store at all times maximized the ability for the store to achieve its sales target, a direct reflection of his ability to succeed as a sales manager. This was his Multiplier Effect.

Having a great team around you will significantly increase your chances of being successful, and I myself have benefitted by being surrounded by good people throughout my life, both personally and professionally. As an example, I played goalkeeper when participating in hockey and soccer and benefitted greatly from having very good teammates. In organized baseball, I preferred back catcher, and having a highly skilled team around me, especially pitchers, made my life so much easier. I consider myself a mediocre keeper in soccer; however, one year, our team was so strong that we barely allowed scoring chances. I won the "Keeper of the Year" award. The trophy was awarded to the keeper on the team who allowed the fewest goals. I was embarrassed receiving the award—I'm quite certain that a rose bush could have won it for our team that year.

If you're a leader in a business environment, assessing your team should be your first order of business. This will determine how successful you, your company and everyone around you will be. Your main responsibility is to motivate everyone to be aligned and move in the same direction. Understand that not everyone will move at the same speed, but they all need to move forward to achieve the strategic plan. The ones who move too slowly or refuse to align with everyone else need to be dealt with immediately—Kill or Cure.

When I was first appointed to SVP of Group Life and Health at Standard Life, our team was divided. Sales, Marketing and Underwriting had a contentious relationship, and it affected our performance. We'd developed a comprehensive and ambitious strategic plan with an accompanying structure and couldn't afford this. After careful consideration, I concluded that we didn't have the right people within our leadership team to complement the plan and structure that we'd developed.

I understood clearly that the Multiplier Effect for success was having the right team in place. I approached our SVP Human Resources with an idea that would initially cause disruption and pain, but I believed that was what was required. Our president was fully supportive.

Within a twenty-four-hour period, I revised our team. It wasn't easy, but it was the right thing to do. I couldn't cure the situation with some of the current people. I had to kill it and start fresh. Simultaneously, I appointed our managers of underwriting, our quotation calculation leadership, to lead our sales operations in each region. No one seemed to understand why I wanted to place our pricing people in sales. They were head office personnel who didn't have sales experience and weren't customer-facing individuals. But it made perfect sense to me. Here's why.

Our sales offices received many requests for proposal each week. The salespeople made sure all of the information required to produce a quotation was included in the material forwarded by their brokers. Then the request went off to our underwriting departments that performed a triage to determine which we'd want to pursue. Our closing ratio, the number of quotes that were produced and sold, was approximately 15 percent at the time. That means, for every one hundred quotes produced, we sold fifteen of them. This ratio applied to just cases quoted that made it through the triage, not received and rejected, of which there were many more and which required much time to assess. Let's think about that for a moment. Imagine how you'd feel if 85 percent of the work you produced as an underwriter was shredded. That's a lot of frustration, wasted time and effort. I reasoned that if we had greater pricing expertise in the sales offices, the initial triage could happen there. The result was more cases rejected at the sales office and fewer moving on to our underwriting department. We produced fewer quotes, but they were of higher quality, and our closing ratios improved. We quoted less and sold more. Our sales offices were happy because their remuneration increased, and our underwriters were more engaged because their efforts were more successful.

With the strong foundation of humanity and a supportive hand from each other, we can achieve the unimaginable.

My First Senior Executive Team

I never seriously considered applying for the position of President and CEO because, quite frankly, it never occurred to me that I'd be a successful candidate. It was a long shot, and life was good leading our health division. Remember, this is an insurance company, and they traditionally prefer actuaries and accountants for leaders; and I'm neither. Besides, one internal candidate was heavily favored and seemingly being set up for the position by the head office. I soon reconsidered. "What do I have to lose?" I thought. If you don't ask, you usually don't receive. As I was the SVP of healthcare, the smallest division in the company, the head office didn't really know me, but they'd be obligated to at least meet me as a courtesy. This would give me an opportunity to let them know me and possibly set myself up to be considered for the job in the future. Upon receiving confirmation of my appointment, the first people I reached out to were colleagues whose buy-in and support I needed to succeed in my new role. I walked over to previous president's assistant, and said, "I would like you to stay and help me. I need you." Diane was aware of literally everything and everyone within the organization and was exceptionally talented. If you're familiar with the vintage television series, *M*A*S*H*, she was the Radar of Standard Life and one of the most important Multiplier Effects to my success as president.

Next was our extremely capable SVP Finance. I'm not a finance person, and I knew that the company was going to go through a process whereby we'd be listed on the London Stock Exchange, the FTSE. Christian needed to be supportive and eventually became one of my most trusted and valuable colleagues.

Our SVP Legal, Penny, was next in line. Like finance, I knew little about the law, let alone the Insurance Act and other governing laws and guidelines within our industry. My meeting with Penny was quick and easy. I had her full support. Half-jokingly, my standing instruction with Penny was, "Keep me out of jail and the company out of the papers!"

> *It is fine to argue, fuss and fight with people who you care about. Just be respectful. When you are done, smile. Then make up.*

Your most important and relied upon direct team members should be the people with the talent that you don't possess. It's important to have a complementary skill set in any environment where teamwork is required. This applies within an executive team, a sales team, a board of directors, a sports team and even a family. I always made sure that I surrounded myself with people who knew much more about their areas of expertise than I did. My executive team consisted of two actuaries, a lawyer, an accountant, an accredited human resource specialist, an MBA and a marketing specialist. We didn't always agree, but I appreciated the different perspectives each person brought to the conversations. Most of the time, we concluded with an agreement and common position on each issue we discussed.

Think of each person within a team as an ingredient required for a favorite recipe. Each element is crucial and provides an important contribution. Don't consider the source of each ingredient. Just buy the best quality available to you. If San Marzano tomatoes are required, does their origin matter? How about mozzarella cheese, basil, salt or extra-virgin olive oil? What's important is the quality of each ingredient, and your responsibility as the creator of this dish is to obtain the best available. If this is your thinking, the Margherita pizza you'll create will be marvelous!

Multiplying for Each Other

While studying at York University, I became quite close with two foreign students. One was Judy from Malaysia and the other Bee Yong from Hong Kong. We coordinated classes in order to be together as much as possible, studied together in the library and helped each other with assignments. Judy was a mathematical genius, and Bee Yong was very proficient at computer science. One of our classes together was called The Business Game. At the beginning of the term, the class was separated into small groups that represented companies. Naturally, we were on the same team. Each of us had a specific role in the company, and the budget was assigned by our professor. Our assignment each week was to complete a report that resembled a strategic plan. We needed to decide how much capital resources were to be allocated to each division and what market segment we wanted to be in. Each company sold the same product, but we needed to decide whether we were going to produce a cheap, mass-marketed version with high volume sales, a higher-end version with greater margin but less volume of sales, or something in between. Each company competed with each other for market share and profits. Our numbers were input into a computer simulation program by our professor, and results were calculated each week. Based on the results, companies adjusted their business plans accordingly. At the end of the term, the company that generated the most profits was declared the winner. Judy, Bee Yong and I would be together, but we needed one more student, and Stuart joined us. Once we knew what roles needed to be filled within the company, we naturally gravitated toward what we did best. Judy was our controller. Bee Yong was our head of IT. Stuart, who was a very personable and a sales-oriented person, was head of marketing, and I was president. The president's role was not as prestigious as you may think. It just meant that I had to author our assignment each week. We realized that we had different skills that complemented each other well. This continued throughout our years together at York. I'd proofread Judy's and Bee Yong's papers; Judy would always check our math, and Bee Yong would contribute wherever she could, usually in computer classes. We were in sync, made a great team and were Multiplier Effects for each other.

Great teams can be constructed for all things in life. Friends can form great teams as can life partners. As long as the whole is greater than the sum of its parts, it's a great team in any environment.

Ahoy, Matey!

Consider the "Michelangelo phenomenon." In psychology, the Michelangelo phenomenon is when close, intimate romantic partners influence each other positively over time. In a sense, like Michelangelo's work, they sculpt and shape each other. One brings out the best in the other and vice versa. This is a positive process that causes people to develop into their best selves.

Finding the right partner is one of the most important decisions that you'll make in your life. Only you can determine what type of life partner works for you. Everyone should have the right to decide and select whom they want to spend time with. What I do suggest, however, is not to just consider qualities in the person that you believe are important and align with your value system. Also, consider qualities in a partner that will help you achieve your best self. They are not always complementary, as in traits that you do not have. Some of the qualities can be similar to yours. As an example, if one person is competitive, having a partner who is also competitive can push you to be your best.

I often wonder what qualities people look for in a person they'd consider having a serious relationship with. The top of your list might include sense of humor, intelligence, a great smile, good looks, kindness and honesty. Do these sound familiar? This is fine, but if you don't have self-awareness, what you *think* you're looking for in someone else is a hit-and-miss proposition because you may miss partners that could help you become your best self.

Having self-awareness means knowing what's needed in a partner to achieve the best you can be as a human being. You'll understand which qualities complement, enrich and enhance yours. Similarly, your qualities should help your partner be joyful and happy. If two people find such qualities in each other, they've found their soulmate and will make an outstanding team.

Ask yourself, how do the qualities that I look for in a person line up with achieving my best self?

I'm All Ears

Once you're surrounded by people you can trust, listen to them. You've selected each and every one to be a part of your life for reasons that make sense to you. Perhaps you've gone through an extensive selection process, or perhaps chemistry exists naturally. At a professional level, you more than likely have assessed their strengths, weaknesses and how all of them, including you, will blend together to form an incredible team. Now is the time to harness all of this and realize the possibilities that lie before you.

Listen to your superiors at work. They're part of your information-gathering process and will be influential in your ability to be your best self. Absorb everything that you can from higher-ranking people you respect within your company. They often will give you great insight that will be useful to you.

Listen to friends, family and strangers. You'll learn a great deal from them. Family elders have a wealth of information that they could share about the family tree, living through difficult times, or even what it was like to watch television for the first time.

I've recently learned much about my father's childhood from my cousins Bill and Angelo, whom I hadn't seen in many years. Their mom relayed stories of her childhood, which included many of my father's. It was fascinating listening to them.

Striking up a conversation with strangers can also be exciting. You can learn a lot about the world.

Now, consider the possibility of listening beyond people. What can you learn from listening to the sounds of nature? A river or stream? How about your pets? The humming of an automobile engine? Wherever and whenever there is sound, there's an opportunity to listen and learn.

Generosity

Sir Sandy Crombie is a leader that I greatly admire. He spent his entire career at Standard Life, beginning as an actuarial student and working his way up to chief executive officer in 2004. He led our international operations from our global headquarters in Edinburgh, Scotland. He preferred to hire people, support them and give them the space to succeed. He didn't tolerate foolishness, was very competitive and expected results. Sandy was a boss.

Every time he visited Canada, usually for board meetings or special events, we'd allocate time to spend together and discuss various topics. He always asked about my family and how I was doing on a personal level before any other topic of discussion. On one such visit, we began talking about my children and what they were up to. I mentioned that they were voracious readers and huge fans of Charlie Fletcher, a well-known author who lives in Scotland. Sandy said that he personally knew Mr. Fletcher! Within a few days of Sandy returning to Scotland, I received a signed copy of *Silvertongue*. Sandy also knew that my wife, Mary, loved cooking, especially Italian dishes. Sandy sent signed copies of two books authored by Mary Contini, another personal friend. Mary Contini is a first-generation Italian Scot. She's an author and director of Valvona & Crolla, a renowned Edinburgh delicatessen, restaurant and cookery school. Sandy always seemed to know someone or have experienced something that was useful for me both personally and professionally. I just listened and learned.

During another visit, he and I were discussing something that I wanted to do within the organization. I wanted to convey a specific message during a presentation to the staff and had a peer review process for presentations and speeches whereby I'd ask some of my team members to review my material. They didn't agree with me on a particular point. I was adamant that I was right about this item but couldn't seem to get the agreement of my executive team. I tried to rationalize my thinking and convince them to see things as I saw them. No luck. I explained this to Sandy. He listened intently, no doubt formed his own opinion, and then reminded me of the classic advice that if everyone keeps telling you to lie down, you're probably drunk, and you should lie down. I adjusted my messaging.

This lesson can be applied all of the time. If several of my friends are in agreement with each other, opposing something that I've done or said, I trust them and realize that they have my best interests in mind. They're more than likely right, and I listen to them.

Fair and Equal

I believe that everyone should always be treated fairly. This is one of our rights as human beings. However, I don't think that everyone should be treated equally all of the time. Some people are just more valuable than others in a particular situation and should be treated, and rewarded, as such. Sports teams do it all of the time. Each team knows who their superstars are, and they're rewarded higher and treated more favorably than other teammates. The rationale is simple. The best players increase fan interest and provide the greatest opportunity to win and generate more income. Everyone plays an important role, but fans are more interested in superstars than other players because they're better at their jobs.

This concept is very important in the workplace as well and applies to each and every employee at any level. Some employees contribute more to an organization than others. It's up to each of us to ensure that we're one of those employees. That's why achieving your maximum potential is so important.

Deserving of More than Maximum

Robert Faille was the head of our Taxation department. He had a tremendous amount of knowledge and experience. Robert loved everything about taxes—federal, provincial, corporate, anything. Whenever a new federal or provincial budget was tabled, by the next day, he knew how it would affect our business and our customers. He alerted all departments that might be affected. This was important because, if the changes affected them, we needed to quickly inform our front-line salespeople, customer service areas, customers and intermediaries. Sometimes, we also needed to update IT systems to accommodate the changes.

Each year, Robert and his team somehow found a way to help us manage our tax burden more efficiently. He'd consult with our external auditors, our regulators and anyone else if he had an idea that could help. Sometimes, his work resulted in significant cost savings for us, which of course, helped our results. Because of the size of our company, a small adjustment could result in a significant number of dollars of corporate tax savings. Robert was remunerated above our maximum salary scale for his position. Each year, during our annual salary review process, Robert was recommended for the highest allowable increase. This placed him even farther from his maximum salary scale. Our Human Resources department was apprehensive about having anyone remunerated significantly above scale and naturally questioned the recommended increase. Like a broken record, each year, I stated clearly, and I quote myself here, "Robert somehow finds ways to help manage our taxes effectively each year. He helps us achieve our profit targets. If we need to give him (whatever figure we were discussing) to reward him annually on his salary, fine. I wish that we had more Robert Failles." He was certainly a Multiplier Effect for us.

Good People Make Mistakes

If you are fortunate to have a good person in your life, forgive their occasional foolishness. They are still a good person, and there are not enough of them out there.

Good people will do silly things on occasion. They'll make mistakes, sometimes minor and sometimes costly. It could be because they took on a little too much, or it could be sheer oversight. If they're good, trusted and valuable, forgive them. Let it go. Too often I've seen goodwill built over months and years of excellent work ruined by the reaction to a mistake. I don't understand it. As long as the errors are neither catastrophic nor repeated, in the grand scheme of things, who cares? They're still good and valuable people. As a matter of fact, you'll gain more loyalty and productivity if this is your approach. Allow people to make mistakes.

This applies to all of life's circumstances. Imagine a friend you've become very close with. You consider them a good person, and you get along very well. You've shared many experiences together and have been supportive of each other. You may even consider them one of your best friends. Now imagine that this person does something that offends you in the form of an insult or an action. They may or may not have done it intentionally. What will be your reaction? Will the insult affect your relationship temporarily? Permanently? Will you never forget what this person said or did? Barring them having done something justifying a total break in the relationship, talk to them and forgive them. There are not enough good people in the world, and if you find one, do what you can to hang onto them.

No Big Deal

Penny was SVP of Legal and Compliance at Standard Life. She and her team always produced excellent work. She is an extremely talented person that I have a tremendous amount of respect for. One day, Penny walked into my office with a face as sad as I've ever seen. "There has been an oversight, and I think that you should know right away," she said. Because I was president in Montreal, the Quebec regulator, the Autorité des marchés financiers (AMF), required that my current address be registered in their files at all times. If I moved, they needed to know, and we had a certain amount of time to inform them, or we'd receive a fine. I changed residence, and somehow her team missed the deadline informing the AMF of my change of address by a few days. As a result, we received a small fine. As mentioned, I have a lot of time and respect for Penny. She was one of the most trusted and competent members of our executive team. Her work ethic, professionalism and sound advice were invaluable. I was not fussed, but Penny felt terrible about the oversight because although not directly responsible, it happened within her team. I smiled. "Penny, it's not a big deal. Will it ever happen again?" "Absolutely not!" was her reply. "Good," I replied. "Let's look at it as a learning experience. Let's not forget it, but let's not worry about it either."

People Are People

In a professional and personal environment, make sure that you get to know people as human beings, not just colleagues or friends. This will have a Multiplier Effect on your relationship and your ability to succeed. Get to know them on a personal level. Take an interest in their families and hobbies. If you genuinely like and respect each other, you'll all be happier, more productive and your relationship will be healthier. If you don't like or respect each other as human beings, you'll just do the minimum of what is expected.

Imagine yourself in any situation where you need to interact with someone else. This could be at home, in the gym, at school or at work. If you like someone you're interacting with, how do you act and respond? Will you do what you can to help them be successful? Will you support them? Will you try to understand them? Will you warn them of potential danger? Will you give your knowledge and the benefit of your experience to them? Of course you will.

People who respect you as a human being will make you aware of your vulnerabilities and the problems you're overlooking. If a train is coming, and you aren't paying attention, they'll warn you. If someone doesn't like you as a leader, friend, colleague, or family member, they may see the train coming, but they may feel no obligation or responsibility to inform you, not caring that it will hit you.

An easy way to develop relationships that are important is to invite those people into your personal space, like your home. It helps you to understand each other as people. And if you have a partner or family, it also provides the opportunity for them to meet those closest to you. I often invited colleagues to my home to meet my family and also enjoyed meeting theirs.

Joseph Who?

When I was first appointed President and CEO of Standard Life, besides employees within my division, Group Life and Health, no one really knew me. Group Life and Health was our smallest unit, and we were located in a separate building in downtown Montreal. I was only in our head office about once a month to attend Executive Committee meetings.

I decided to create a biweekly newsletter called *Online with Joseph*. It gave me the opportunity to communicate what was happening within our company, but more importantly, it let everyone know who I was as a person. I wrote about my family, hobbies, what books were on the reading list and so on. Over time, the newsletter became our most successful communication vehicle within Standard Life. Most read it and looked forward to the next edition. If Human Resources wanted our employees to know something, it was included in the newsletter. It evolved from being my personal communication medium to everyone's newsletter.

We also included personal stories of our employees. Standard Life had a tradition of gifting pendants or pins to employees celebrating their twenty-fifth anniversary with us. They'd select their preference, and I'd spend some time in my office chatting with them and presenting their gift, always asking what it was like at the company twenty-five years prior. Responses were similar for the most part. Stories of departments sharing one telephone, the first telecopier and the first fax machine were common.

Then I asked the important questions. Given a choice, what would you be doing right now? What are you passionate about? This is where I discovered the real information I was seeking, the

"Who are You?" question. I wanted to know what characteristics made them unique human beings. Responses were as varied as can be. One employee was an accomplished puppeteer, complete with a website. He was a virtual encyclopedia of knowledge about puppets. He knew their history, cultural significance within societies, sizes, types and materials used in their making. He was impressive. We had many want-to-be chefs, bakers and gardeners. Another employee had a passion for traveling to exotic locations alone. She considered herself somewhat of an introverted and private person and preferred the isolation of solo travel. Once she arrived at her destination, she became a different person. She avoided other tourists and immersed herself within the local people and customs. She explained that this was the only way to truly appreciate the experience, and I agreed.

We produced *Online with Joseph* for most of my tenure as CEO, and my 150th double edition was my last, a farewell letter to everyone.

Linked Together

We are all a part of multiple teams at a macro and micro level, and we rely on each other for success. At a macro level, we're a part of a team that's composed of all living things. We all form a part of a universal energy, and in every aspect of life, each of us is linked with every form of life. This is a team that we'll be a part of forever. On a micro level, we belong to many teams, including those at work and home, some of which are long-term, like family, and others that will be more temporary.

Always surround yourself with good people and identify yourself as someone who is not only striving to be their best, but is also, as part of this process, making everyone around them better. Being part of a successful team will ensure that the whole is always greater than the sum of its parts. Be each other's Multiplier Effect. This is what links us all together.

CHAPTER 10

People Are Everything

Hired on Intuition

Soon after becoming manager of the Standard Life sales office in Toronto, we were left without a sales assistant because the predecessor coaxed his assistant to join him at his new employer. We managed with temporary help until I decided whom to hire as my full-time assistant. It would have been an easy transition for our office to keep the temporary employee, but instead I hired Gino, a young immigrant from the Philippines who would come to our office for a couple of hours at night to type sales proposals and renewals. I admired Gino's commitment and positive attitude. "Trust your instincts," I said to myself. Gino's work was excellent, always going beyond what was required of his position and he eventually became leader of the administrative team in the office.

I've always believed that hiring the best people available is a company's best strategy for success. Skillset, education and experience are of course important and serve as the minimum requirements for consideration in any position. Beyond that, a company should select people who have integrity and good values, are empathetic, have a strong work ethic and overall good character. Companies should hire people who are excellent human beings. I've always believed that excellent people can overcome and make up for a lot of bad things, including structural flaws and technology deficiencies. They are a Multiplier Effect for success.

> *Search for people who are naturally excellent because one cannot teach excellence in people*

Fast Followers

Many markets, including Canada, have major industry segments that are oligopolistic in nature, whereby a few companies control and influence pricing, products, service and often governmental policy within their industries. This includes banks as well as insurance, gas, electricity, grocery, internet, cable and mobile phone companies. This means that the market is commoditized for the most part and needs to be creative to distinguish itself from competition. Job descriptions and salary scales are similar within companies in similar industries. As an example, a disability claims adjudicator in one insurance company basically does the same job as a disability claims adjudicator in another insurance company and is paid within the same salary scales. Other examples are bank tellers and receptionists. Most companies also use the same handful of consultants to determine salary scales for their employees. Products and services within the large companies are similar, and if one company introduces something new, other companies become fast followers, quickly imitating their competition. Services and technology are also similar, and often suppliers provide the same technology to multiple companies within an industry. As you can see, there is plenty of similarity within these large industries.

At Standard Life, I viewed this as an advantage. Since products, services, technology and pricing within our industry were similar and easily copied, we decided to make our people our most inimitable competitive advantage. Strategically, we focused on being excellent in some aspect within each line of business and good enough to compete everywhere else; we decided our people would be our Multiplier Effect for success. Let's take the example of the disability claims adjudicator above. If our adjudicators were more empathetic and more creative in finding return-to-work solutions for disabled employees, working closely with treating physicians and employers, our results would be more favorable than our competitors. This translates to employees returning to work sooner, increasing customer satisfaction, and ultimately greater financial success for everyone.

The position of receptionist is one of the most important jobs in any company in my opinion. Generally, the basic duties of receptionists are similar in any workplace. As the initial point of contact with customers, they're often responsible for the first impression of the company. What is your first impression if you encounter a receptionist who is unhelpful or disinterested in their job or one who is pleasant and genuinely interested in making certain that your inquiry is handled in a satisfactory manner? This would be a much more favorable experience. The job descriptions may be similar, but the people are different.

Another good example is the salesperson. A salesperson's success depends on managing the relationship between the buyer and the company they represent. If products, pricing and servicing within their respective industry were similar, how the salesperson managed these two relationships would determine how successful they were. I'm convinced that customers trust the individuals they deal with more than the companies they represent. Most successful salespeople not only have excellent sales skills but are also empathetic, understanding and flexible enough to manage multiple relationships at the same time.

Can you remember a time when you encountered an uninterested or not very useful salesperson? Do you remember your best sales or service experience?

All of the above are examples of excellent people making a difference, and each of us has the ability to be the same. As individuals, we have multiple roles to play within society. We can be a co-worker, a friend, a student, a family member. The circumstances are uniquely ours. With complete self-awareness, we understand who we are and what characteristics make us unique individuals. These characteristics are the building blocks that form the foundation of who we are as people. It's up to us to ensure that our authentic personal brand is reflective of being an excellent person, and hence, our best self. Being an excellent human being will complement your natural and learned skills and will serve as a Multiplier Effect for you.

People are your most non-easily imitated competitive advantage.

The Most Promising People

At Standard Life, I was always interested in knowing who we considered our most outstanding people. One day, I asked for a list of our most promising employees—a list that was generated during the annual reviews process. These were people we'd keep an eye on for promotions and future development. Some were part of our succession planning exercise as well. I met with Human Resources to go through the list. Our discussion initially focused on how long each employee had been with Standard Life, how long they'd been in their current position, which departments they worked at and what their experience was. This was useful, but it wasn't the information I was looking for. I needed to know how good they were.

We shouldn't determine the quality of employees based on the length of time they've been in their roles. Tenure shouldn't be the major consideration as to whether someone is ready for a promotion or new responsibilities. The assumption is that they're well experienced and can be ready for new challenges. This can be true but isn't always the case. Having a skill set that is fit for purpose and appropriate for the job is more important. People with talent that can't be easily learned or replicated by others are highly valuable. This includes all of us! We all have natural skills that others don't. Conversely, others have unique natural skills that we don't. This is the beauty of being a human being. It's important for us and everyone to be keenly aware of what our unique natural strengths are. They are the foundation for our success, and others will notice.

I'm impressed with the excellent talent that is all around us and available to every employer, especially the young talent. At Standard Life, if we found someone we believed could be a contributor to our success, we'd try to hire them, even if there was no current job opening. We would "park" them somewhere knowing that, as an organization with more than two thousand people, there would be a position open at some point to place them in. I learned to never underestimate the importance of stockpiling excellent, talented people.

Investing in yourself is a lifelong proposition. This includes looking for learning and training opportunities everywhere, especially within the workplace. Excellent employers will offer many programs for employees to further their expertise, promote well-being and enhance promotion possibilities. They're not worried about how long you may or may not stay with the company. They understand that there are too many future possibilities to consider, and most don't unfold as anticipated anyway. Some people like to "resume pad" by having their current employers pay for education and training that will make them more marketable to other employers. This won't be of concern to an excellent employer because they realize that it's their responsibility to advance the careers and potential of each employee, and they have an obligation to ensure that there are interesting job opportunities available for everyone. Their thinking is that no matter how long someone stays in their job, as long as they are contributing and offering value to the organization, it's fine. This could be for one, ten or even twenty years.

This principle applies to you as well. Don't necessarily think about how long you'll stay with an employer. The future holds too many variables and possibilities. Work on learning as much as you can and advancing through all of the opportunities that lie before you. It's important to find an employer that is supportive of you and your growth potential because it will have a Multiplier Effect on your career.

Don't look for a perfect fit. Trust yourself and the universe to find the pieces of the puzzle that align not perfectly, but just right.

The Big Two

Two of the most important characteristics a person can have are integrity and honesty in my opinion. Integrity is the practice of being honest and adhering to strong ethical values and moral principles. A lack of integrity reflects a flawed human being. Having strong moral principles means that, for the most part, you'll always do the right thing and with honest intent. It takes a strong person to always do what is right, especially under duress, when the alternative may be easier and more widely accepted or is more advantageous. This applies to all situations in life, whether personal or professional. Do you remember when we first spoke about the Law of Cause and Effect in Chapter 4? It suggests that what you give is what you get, positive or negative. Conducting yourself with integrity in an honest manner will result in positive energy flowing and positive things happening for you. This is a sign of a person well on their way to being their best self.

Anyone Can Help

Everyone, always, should be treated with dignity and respect. On a broad scale, we're all one energy, sharing our world and universe. Therefore, in a sense, if you're discourteous or disrespectful to someone, you're being disrespectful and discourteous to yourself.

As a group insurance salesperson, I required the trust and confidence of my brokers to attain my sales objectives. Competition with other salespeople and other companies was fierce. Being visible and vying for their attention was important, but it was often difficult to arrange meetings with them. Maintaining good relationships with their executive assistants was important because they controlled the brokers' calendars, and if they liked you, they'd always find a way to squeeze you in for a meeting. I made it a point to carry promotional items in the trunk of my car to hand out to executive assistants whenever visiting their offices. I was always respectful of their time and of them as human beings. These were very important people and facilitated access to my brokers, which in turn helped me to achieve my sales objectives. If I needed to see a broker to explain a sales proposition or a company position, I was usually able to obtain a few minutes of their time, even if their agenda was full. Their executive assistant arranged it for me. If you treat everyone with equal respect and emit positive energy, good things happen.

Everyone is important, and we all need to rely on each other if we're going to succeed in being our best. This sounds familiar, I know, but we don't always think this way unfortunately. The hierarchy within workplaces offers another good example. People with positions that are deemed less influential or further down the salary scale are sometimes viewed less favorably than others with "more important" jobs. Their roles and opinions are often dismissed. This isn't fair, and those that don't realize this will miss opportunities.

Don't Lose Your Sense of Wonder

Another one of my favorite words is *wonder*. I marvel at children's astonishment and excitement upon discovering something new, unexpected and beautiful. As adults, we can have this same sense of wonder if we choose to, but for various reasons, most of us are conditioned to suppress it. Can you imagine what our learning experiences would be like if everyone maintained their sense of wonder? Wonder is infinite. There are no internal or external elements of wonder. It doesn't have a sense of time or space. It's a feeling that touches all of our senses. We can wonder how a fruit tastes, how the fur of a pet feels and what the smell of a new perfume is. We can wonder about the view from the top of the

Himalayas or about the beautiful crying sound a newborn baby makes. We can wonder what someone is thinking or how someone sings beautifully. Wonder is different from visualization and has a natural element of innocent curiosity. We can have a sense of wonder every time we look at something or someone, even if it's for the hundredth time.

Looking at something with an absence of wonder, we see what we want to see. We see what we believe we should be seeing. We tint our views with what suits our purpose. If we want to see what's actually there and come back to wonder, we need to disregard our memory of past experiences and learning. Choosing to leave our memories behind, we're completely present and approach each moment as if it were new, experiencing a sense of wonder each time. Let's try an experiment. I warn you though, this may take a few times to get used to!

If you have a partner in your life or someone you're very close to, the next time you see or interact with them, look at them. Observe carefully what it is that you're seeing. Now, try to forget about your past with them and observe them with a sense of wonder. Look at them again as if for the first time. Don't look at them through tinted lenses forged in memory. Now, describe to them in detail what you see. Notice their features, their expressions, how they move, their mannerisms and their voice. If you maximize your ability to be your truest best self, you're able to see clearly without a tinted viewpoint and view them with a sense of newness. If you control your tints, you'll have access to a sense of wonder.

Let's try another exercise.

Wherever you are reading this, look around and select an object. What do you see? Look more carefully. Don't just look, but observe. Write down what you see and describe it in detail below:

_____

_____

_____

_____

_____

_____

_____

Now, can you learn something new from viewing the object from a new and different perspective? Perhaps see what is not obviously visible?

As I write this, I'm glancing out of my office window, observing the wind blowing through trees in my backyard. I can see how different branches from different trees sway with different range. I wonder why they sway in this manner, direction and range. I wonder what the root system of the tree looks like, and how broad and extensive it must be. I see birds selecting one branch over another. I again wonder why they select that particular one and not another. I see some leaves falling off of trees, but others do not. Why? Squirrels are climbing trees with speed and agility. How and why? I wonder.

Reawaken your natural sense of wonder and enhance your interaction with everyone and everything around you. Be your own inimitable competitive advantage, and be the person that you admire being around. Most of all, be an excellent person. This is a powerful Multiplier Effect.

CHAPTER 11

Good Leaders

Good leaders share similar traits, they:
- are completely self-aware
- encourage people to be their best
- understand that their role is to make your role easier
- understand the power of their words
- give people space and room to grow
- allow mistakes
- stretch people beyond their limits
- give people influence
- respect others' opinions
- are honest and trustworthy
- are readers and learners
- have an acute strategic vision
- are politically astute
- have empathy
- always strive to be better
- always share knowledge

- are humble enough to know when they need help
- are consistent in their decision-making and actions
- are genuinely interested in people's well-being
- are inspiring and have an uncanny ability to motivate people to be their best

I state these early so you can reflect on them throughout this chapter. Generally, a team is a group of people bound together by an over-arching objective of achieving a common goal. They work together either dependently or interdependently, and each team member plays a key role in overall success. We are all members of various teams on a personal or professional basis, and everything we discuss in this chapter can apply to both worlds. In one way or another, we are all leaders and valuable contributors for teams at work, home or among friends.

If you are a leader of a team, you need to make sure that you give everyone ample space and support to do their best. Consider what they know as an extension of what you know. If your team is truly ready to be greater than the sum of its parts, it's time to create an environment to foster success for them. Move out of their way. A strong leader realizes that their primary duty isn't to perform the functions of their team, but to support and facilitate everyone to achieve the best they're capable of. If your team is personal in nature, like a family or recreational team, enjoy all that everyone has to offer; be in the wonder of seeing them all as they are and seeing what everyone can bring to make each experience memorable. Learn and grow together.

I was often asked, "What type of leader are you?" and "How would you define your leadership style?" I never knew how to respond to these questions because I usually adapted to what I believed was appropriate in the circumstances, and I encourage you to do the same. Don't label yourself with a specific style. As soon as you do this, you and your colleagues will be psychologically bound to it, and you'll begin to believe that you need to act and react in certain ways to justify your label. This is a trap that needs to be avoided. Your leadership style is unique to you. As a clever human being with sincere and noble intentions and good intuition, you'll always know how to act and don't need a label to define what that is. Seminars, books or other mediums that promote specific styles are excellent for information purposes, but not necessarily for adoption. Many are a reflection of the current market environment or the experiences of specific people in specific circumstances. I prefer to examine any situation with neutrality, assess what's required based on what's evident, and adapt accordingly. This approach isn't a management style in as much as it's simply conducting yourself in a manner that brings about the best in people to achieve common objectives.

I'm amused when it's suggested that different generations need to be handled differently. Baby Boomers, Generation X's, Millennials, Generation Z's, and Generation Alpha's do not need to be managed differently from one another. This is a generalization that isn't productive. We may have been born in different decades and eras, but we're all still human beings with similar needs, and for the most part, share similar values. Besides our core needs of air, food, water and shelter, we all crave connection, certainty and growth. We all want to make a difference and contribute in some way. Let's not look at each other as people of certain generations, but just simply as people. Let's remember that everyone is responsible for being their best self, and you, as a person in their life, leader or otherwise, are responsible for helping them achieve this. You'll naturally do the right thing because, remember, if you know who to be, you'll know what to do.

Harnessing the Power of the Collective

An important element in maximizing your potential as a good leader is understanding how to harness the power of the collective team to help attain common goals. I've always believed that if you put several people in a room together to discuss an issue, they'll eventually come up with a solution or plan of action. Sometimes it may take longer, but I find that it always works out well. I apply this principle all of the time. If someone came into my office with a problem, I rarely offered a solution. "Let's sit down and talk about it," were my first words, and off we went. People with the same ultimate objective of resolving the issue are usually quite pleased to discuss their views and appreciate the opportunity for input. This simple concept doesn't just apply to the business environment but to any situation that requires a resolution.

Corporate team-building exercises are another example. These were created for groups of individuals to put their minds together to find solutions to solve puzzles, discover clues and find their way out of a "problem." Success is dependent on everyone discussing various approaches and working in unison. This is a brilliant way to spend time with people as well as a great exercise for the brain.

Sometimes, people will have differing opinions when discussing a resolution to an issue. Even though the end goals are the same, how to reach them may differ. I prefer this to a unanimous decision that's arrived at in haste. This is usually a sign that there hasn't been enough discussion or consideration. Sometimes, the group wants to make a decision quickly and move on. My preferred approach is to look at different perspectives. This usually leads to more effective resolutions. This also means compromise.

Generally, compromise is viewed as a negative term. A compromise solution is one in which no one party completely receives what they desire. Decisions made in compromise for the good of the whole are excellent. These are Appropriate for Now decisions, and I don't view them as not achieving what's ultimately wanted, but as something that offers the best outcome that accommodates everyone, which is important. If decisions are made on this basis, you rarely need to worry about winning battles because the war will naturally be won—reaching consensus is the "win." Compromise, if agreed to in good faith, is often the best solution and the result of harnessing the power of the collective to achieve a common end result.

Engagement

We've discussed how people are the most important assets for a company. At Standard Life, we monitored our employee engagement levels through surveys each year. I was proud that our scores increased each year for all of the seven years that my executive team was together. However, we were envious of other organizations with higher scores. One of our leading national newspapers conducted a yearly survey to determine the top fifty most engaged workplaces in Canada, and we wanted Standard Life to be on that list.

I did what I thought was the most logical thing at the time. I wrote a letter to all of the fifty CEOs of the companies that made the list the previous year and requested a meeting, in person or by telephone, to discuss what they were doing to have such an engaged workforce. We received a response from a great majority of them, mostly because they were wondering what we were up to. I simply stated that I wanted to replace them one day on the survey and that I needed to know what they were doing specifically to have happy and engaged employees. Many shared their experiences as I shared mine, and we learned a great deal from each other. We implemented several new initiatives as a result of these discussions, which helped our engagement levels continue to trend upward. We were never able to make the timing work to participate in the national survey, but I'm glad that we were able to speak to all of the companies that we spoke to. The CEOs were generous with their time, passionate about their employees and candid with their remarks.

It's important to respect all opinions in your information-gathering process to decision-making, but always consider the source. You need to respect informed opinions more than uninformed ones. I know, this sounds logical, but sometimes uninformed people are very good at falsely demonstrating an informed view. These are con artists, and we discuss this topic in greater detail in Chapter 12. Also, sometimes very smart people say stupid things. This is because they believe that they are smart enough to have informed opinions on topics they don't know much about. They apply their knowledge of one thing to another and assume that it works. It sometimes does but often doesn't. Always weigh the opinion of someone who has more experience more than someone who is theorizing. Finally, remember that advice and opinion can play a part in how you make decisions but shouldn't make the decision for you.

Have Your "Go-To" People Lined up

Good leaders know when to ask for help and have certain people they rely upon on a regular basis. These are trusted friends, family and colleagues that receive the first call when something needs to be done or discussed. They're considered go-to for a reason—they always deliver. I've been fortunate to have many great team members be primary points of contact. As a member of any team, personal or professional, we should all strive be a go-to person. The principle can be applied almost anywhere to ensure positive results.

Keith to the Rescue

Keith is my neighborhood go-to person. Keith is a retired mason and is extremely handy. I'm convinced that he can operate and fix any machinery, and when in need of assistance with a project at home, I consult with him. If my lawnmower stops working, Keith knows what's wrong. Does anyone know how to mix concrete? Call Keith! His stories are always entertaining, and best of all, our consultation usually ends with him brushing me aside and actually doing most of the work. I'm not sure whether it's because he's very friendly or just doesn't trust me with the task. Either way, I'm so grateful to have Keith around.

As a salesperson, it was important for my success to have a good relationship with many departments, including Marketing, Underwriting, Customer Services and Claims. Smooth and seamless exchanges between these departments meant that our clients were serviced well. There was a defined procedure for communication and decision-making within each one that I couldn't always understand as an impatient salesperson. My solution to this time-consuming bureaucracy was to find a "Keith" in each department. If I had an issue, I contacted them, and they lobbied on my behalf within their area to help resolve the problem. They were an important Multiplier Effect for my success.

Find the Fault

One day, I came up with a game called "Find the Fault." It's a simple game where someone produces an idea and whoever is around is tasked with finding its fault. As an example, during our executive team meetings, an idea was tabled by anyone free of any consideration of restrictions or boundaries. Sometimes, the idea didn't make sense initially, but that didn't stop us. In my case, this process usually began with me brainstorming with myself. This is something I often do to come up with ideas without taking any potential restrictions into consideration. Then, I'd explain my idea and ask the team to find the fault with it. If, during the course of our discussion, the idea was found to have a fault that was fatal, it was abandoned. If the fault wasn't fatal and could be overcome, we decided whether it was worth pursuing further. If the idea didn't have a fault, then it was a good one, and we adopted it. Simple, but effective.

I play Find the Fault all of the time, especially on a personal basis. It helps to foster discussion, consider all possibilities, and guide in whether to pursue an idea or not. It'll work anytime that you think about something and want to solicit other opinions. It's not a process whereby you write down the positives and negatives about an idea, and based on this, a decision is made. With Find the Fault, you always initially assume that an idea is good.

As an example, let's say that you're thinking about buying a new car. Before doing so, play Find the Fault with friends, family or even a mentor. If the faults discussed are fatal, don't pursue it. If they're small or can be overcome reasonably, seriously consider it. If there are no faults at all, go for it! The key is to have no preconceived limitations or restrictions. This can apply to any decision. Simply suggest a thought or idea with an approach that considers no limitations or boundaries, ask people to find the fault, and have fun with what everyone comes up with! Let's play together using the same example above; let's consider the possibility that you're thinking about buying a new car. I'll get us started, and you can complete the list.

Is it time for a new car?

Find the Fault(s)
1. New cars are too expensive
2. I will lease a car
3. I will buy a car
4. I will buy/lease a gas-powered car
5. I will buy/lease a hybrid car

6. I will buy/lease an electric car
7. _____
8. _____
9. _____
10. _____

If you consider any of the above unresolvable, and hence fatal, then you won't be able to buy a new car. As an example, if you can't afford a new car because the type that you need is too expensive, then the fault is fatal. This is only to be considered when all options for resolution are exhausted. In this instance, can the fault be overcome in the form of a loan from a family member? Is there a way to reduce expenses to help with monthly payments? If not, then the fault is fatal. If you can get through all of the potential faults and find solutions for them, congratulations, you're on your way to buying a new car!

Good Leaders Provide Safety Nets and Air Cover

Growing up, I had several friends about the same age on our street. The oldest, Pat, was the alpha dog. He had a bit of a quick temper but never did anything that got out of hand. Pat was just one year older than me. We managed to get along but were very competitive with each other. We'd race to determine who was fastest and would see who could hit a baseball farther. Others within our group would support Pat or me whenever some kind of choice needed to be made, like which partners to select when playing hide and seek. Our schools of choice defined most allegiances. The ones that went to the local public school were pretty close. The others, like myself, attended the local Catholic school and formed a second group. We all found a way to hang out together on the street. One day, Pat and I got into a fight that began with a friendly wrestling match but soon turned into a legitimate fistfight. Pat was stronger and ended up on top of me. Through the corner of my eye, I saw my dad approaching us. I thought, "Whew, I'm going to be rescued" but that's not what my dad had in mind. He just watched as we fought. Panicking, I became more aggressive and kept punching while still lying on my back with Pat on top of me. Finally, my dad pulled Pat away and stopped the fight. Everyone went home. "Dad, why didn't you stop the fight earlier? You saw that Pat was on top and pummeling away at me." He just smiled and said, "You were doing okay. If he was really going to hurt you, I would have pulled him off. Besides, you need to learn how to fight and that being at the bottom of a pile, even a pile of two, is not a good place to be." My dad let me fight, while being my safety net.

As a leader, I believe that you should give your team enough space to manage their responsibilities and give them the proper tools and resources to maximize their ability. Once you've done this, let them go off and perform their duties and responsibilities. Make it very clear that you have faith in them and that you'll be their safety net if they stumble. Let them understand that they can make bold decisions, and you'll support them as you encourage them to try new things. Allow them to make an occasional bad decision as long as it's made with good intention. Missteps are a part of learning. If they know that you'll provide a safety net in the event of failure, it'll give them the confidence to take appropriate risks, which in turn will lead to rewards. If people don't believe they'll have support during times of failure, they'll make conservative decisions, usually to preserve their jobs or reputations, and will never reach the heights of creativity and innovation that they're capable of. Nor will they become their best selves. At home, if you give your partner and children space and create an environment for success for them, and they know that you'll cushion any fall they may have, they'll have the freedom to make bolder decisions and be their best selves.

I've had the fortune of having air cover for most of my life, people higher up the hierarchy in my professional and personal life to watch over me. For you, this could be a boss that wants you to succeed and is careful about protecting you from obstacles that may hurt your success or progress. It could also be a family member that has taken a special interest in you. Perhaps they are a lawyer and know that you want to study law or are a godparent and have a sense of responsibility for your well-being. These people kind of fly over your life at a high altitude, and with this elevated view, they can see what you're up to and offer support if needed. Having air cover helps give you the confidence to make decisions knowing you have their support.

The Power of Someone Else's Belief in You

At Standard Life, we hired Michèle to be in charge of our Health and Wellness unit in 2001. We created a separate unit that focused on our overall client base, but specifically our disability division. The disability portion of our business was beginning to take on greater importance as more and more people were affected by illness, especially mental health. This affected our company and our customers. We viewed this as an opportunity to improve our approach to this business. Most of the industry was focused on early intervention as a means to reduce the duration of disability claims. At Standard Life, we wanted to have claimants return to work as quickly as possible, of course, but we also wanted to prevent the disability in the first place. This was Michèle's area of expertise, and she did excellent work.

When we required a VP of External Communications and Public Affairs, I asked Michèle to take the job. Initially, she was reluctant about her experience matching the role. "This is not forever," I suggested. "I know that it's not your ideal job, but we need someone to handle an important project for a period of time, and the best person for that is you. Once it's finished, we can revisit your responsibilities." I had great faith in Michèle's ability to adapt. I knew that if she was unsure of something, she'd use all of our resources to get the information necessary to carry out her duties. I knew that any completed work would be as close to perfect as it could be. I was Michèle's air cover to make sure that she wouldn't fail in her new responsibilities. She agreed to take the role, and as expected, was excellent.

On occasion, you'll need to take on responsibilities and duties that you don't believe you can handle, but someone else believes in you. Good leaders realize this and will stretch you to limits that you don't believe you can reach. They'll provide both air cover and a safety net for you. If you trust them, trust yourself. These experiences help you grow.

Excellent communication skills are important for everyone. Each of us needs to understand our role in effective communication. If you need to say something several times to someone, and they still don't understand, they're not the problem, you are. You're not communicating with them in a manner that they understand. This is your primary responsibility if you want to convey a message. This is more than likely because you don't know the audience to which you're speaking. To help me with my team, I kept a list of all of their top strengths as assessed by a consulting firm on my desk . Whenever I had a meeting with any of them, I re-read their strengths beforehand and adopted my communication style accordingly.

We had a very diverse group of executives at Standard Life and had all kinds of education and expertise represented around our team table. Even though we all spoke English, we each spoke a different version of English. We had "Actuarial English," "Legal English," "Marketing English," "Accounting English" and "Human Resources English." Each expert had their own English "dialect," and if each spoke a strict version of their English lingo, only their own kind would understand. Have you ever heard two lawyers speaking with each other, or have you ever read a legal document drafted for another lawyer? A translation to regular English is required for the masses to understand. Because of this, I always asked the team to dumb it down so that everyone would understand.

Communication Is the Key

The communication channels within Standard Life were very linear. Communication was delivered from top to bottom. Our executives delivered messages to their managers, who delivered them to their teams and so on. Each level of management was expected to understand the messages being communicated, and it was their responsibility to relay them accurately. This worked well in some divisions, was inconsistent in others and didn't work at all in some. We relied on all of our managers to communicate accurate messages to their teams in a timely manner, especially when we needed to give information to everyone at the same time. This didn't always happen, and results from our employee surveys revealed their frustration. Then, our internal communications unit had an idea to help me.

We were fortunate to have a talented and well-equipped design studio that supported all of our communication efforts. We decided that, when a message needed to be delivered to everyone, they'd videotape me, and the video would be uploaded on our intranet for all of our employees to see. In this manner, everyone had access to the same message at the same time. This type of communication was more timely and effective and, perhaps most importantly, more consistent. It developed into a regularly used vehicle for conveying company information. Our employees embraced and appreciated this form of communication.

Standard Life's Canadian head office was located in Montreal. A great majority of our employees were Francophone, and French was their primary language. Most had a working knowledge of English. I was Anglophone and didn't speak French. Despite this, I don't recall any situation where the language barrier was insurmountable. Most of the time, my French colleagues were the ones doing the heavy translation work, but one way or another, we understood each other. Sometimes I took advantage of the fact that Italian and French are similar and used an Italian word to help. Communication was the key, not necessarily proper pronunciation. This is important. Don't worry too much about perfect grammar or pronunciation when communicating in different languages if you or the person that you're conversing with are not fluent. Technology advancements have made it easier to overcome language barriers, but for the most part, for informal communication, don't stress over needing to be perfect. If you want to communicate something, you'll find a way. My mom had a neighbor who only spoke Spanish and because my mom speaks Italian and some English, she spoke Italian to her neighbor, and her neighbor spoke Spanish to her. While it was not perfect, they understood each other.

Don't Confuse the Message with Too Many Words

A mentor once told me, "Joseph, when you are asked a question or to explain something, always offer only a paragraph. Speak of the chapter only when specifically asked to do so. Never recite the book." This has resonated with me ever since. Use the smallest number of words necessary to make your point. Any more is a waste of time. Also, remember that a great communicator is someone who makes a difficult concept easily understandable, and a poor communicator is someone who makes a simple concept difficult to understand. Poor communicators often use too many words.

Don't Turn up the Volume, Please

I'm convinced that my dad mastered what he considered to be the universal translator—turn up the volume! My dad spoke Italian and just enough English to get by. When my dad had a problem conveying a message and I wasn't around to help him, he turned up the volume. That was his solution. He repeated whatever he'd said, usually in very broken English mixed with Italian, still incomprehensible to the person that he was speaking to, but just said it louder. If the person still didn't understand, he repeated it once again, and once again, louder and louder! He knew exactly what he was doing and somehow, he always ended up getting his message across. This is too embarrassing for me to try, but hey, it worked for him!

I Hate to Say I Told You So

As I grow older and more mature, I realize that the best life advice I've received is by observing and listening to other people. I watch what they do and how they act and incorporate whatever wisdom they share into my life. Parents and grandparents are great leaders, and their experiences and knowledge are especially useful. Children usually respect their grandparents, however, they seem to treat their parents differently throughout their life stages. Parents often go through three phases in their children's eyes. When they're young, they consider their parents to be the smartest people in the world. Phase two begins in their preteen and teenage years where they consider their parents naive and not as liberal or cool as their friends' parents. Next is phase three when, in their twenties, children come to the realization that their parents were right all along and are now geniuses. This realization usually comes after several mistakes are made against the opinion or judgment of their parents. I learned early that when my mom, a great leader herself, suggested something, she was almost always right. If my mom thought I should take an umbrella to school because it was going to rain, I should take an umbrella. Sunshine and cloudless skies meant nothing. If Mom said it was going to rain, it usually did.

Ultimately, time-tested principles that can be applied in life will always be effective and relevant and will help you be a good leader. These principles can come from anywhere: religious literature, cultural customs or people. Watch and listen to anyone that you admire and who has proven to be successful. What they're doing and have done in the past may not fit your circumstance, but a variation can. You just need to adapt the principles to what you require. This is why I'm drawn to the yogic way of being, as described in Chapter 2, adapted to my individual preferences in both personal and professional life. This way of being is thousands of years old and still relevant today.

Good Leaders as a Multiplier Effect

If you're fortunate enough to work for or associate with a great leader that you respect and admire, observe and learn as much as you can from them. You'll take some of those teachings with you as you continue on your path to greatness. This works in all aspects of life. You'll also probably be a much more productive person if you're working for a great leader given the happiness factor. You'll do better work and apply greater effort if you like your boss. A good leader will create an environment where you'll consistently be at your best.

Let's refer back to the list at the beginning of this chapter and reconsider all of the similar traits that good leaders share. Each of these traits is a Multiplier Effect. We're all leaders in one capacity or another. Some lead people within companies while others lead teams or families. Most importantly, you lead your own path to become the best person that you can be and thus are a leader of yourself.

Now, list what you think are the most important traits of a good leader. How many of them apply to you? Remember, we're all leaders in our own way, at work or at home.

_____

_____

_____

_____

_____

_____

_____

_____

_____

_____

_____

_____

Are you pleased and surprised at your choices? Don't be. You're an amazing person and leader.

CHAPTER 12

Bad Leaders

Like good leaders, most bad or incompetent leaders also share similar traits. Remember, these traits can apply in professional and personal life. These people:

- do not select who they associate with well—usually only people who agree with them
- drive away good people, especially when they are recently appointed as leaders
- are insecure
- are bullies
- micromanage, usually due to control and trust issues
- play favorites
- have an inability to listen
- never get 100 percent effort from employees
- have no empathy
- hate to be challenged
- do not encourage constructive and creative dialogue
- are not coachable

- are selfish
- are influenced by rumors and innuendo
- like to take credit for positive things and are quick to blame for negative things

Have you ever worked for a bad boss or poor leader? Have you ever had a terrible teacher or a horrible coach? How did you perform? How did you feel? Not so great, I would bet.

Undisciplined Gunslinger

Have you ever had a boss who must have graduated from Horrible University of Leadership and Management? If not, you're lucky! This type of leader usually causes chaos and discord within the team and staff. They will ride into a meeting like an undisciplined gunslinger, shoot everything in sight, and then leave everyone behind to clean up the mess. It works for them because they remind everyone who is boss, and they feel as if they are somehow accomplishing something. These leaders have many attributes that are counterproductive. Sometimes they are inconsistent, quick-tempered, and bullies. Within a brief period many people will leave the company, because bad leaders often drive away good people or replace them with their own hires that they prefer. This can cost a company valuable knowledge and experience. What should you do if you find yourself in such a circumstance?

In my family, we have a saying that applies perfectly in such situations: Contento e fesso (Happy and fooled.) That's what you should do. If your boss hates to be challenged, even with logic and rules of law, and their rants often derail meetings, make them happy and fooled. Adopt a new strategy. Stop questioning them when they discuss doing things that are, in your opinion, irrational, counterproductive or impossible. Just provide all of the necessary information and reports that are required, and when they go off on one of their rants or tangents that threaten to hijack the agenda, just listen. When the meeting is over, go back to your business. Build a network of support with other colleagues elsewhere and bypass your boss whenever possible. Never compromise and make sure the quality of your work is always exceptional. Whenever I myself was in such a situation, I always found a way to work productively and continue to achieve optimum performance.

So how do you deal with bad bosses when you still love your job? Outsmart them. I've been fortunate to not have had too many horrible bosses or leaders in my personal and professional life. Most have been very supportive and have helped me achieve things that sometimes seemed impossible. However, there were a few instances where high performance was expected despite ineffective leadership. Just be cleverer than them to deal with those situations.

There are many ways to outsmart a toxic leader. One of the strategies that worked best for me was to focus on my responsibilities; not on their words or actions that were detrimental to me or my team's performance. Reminding myself of what my primary duties were and to whom I was ultimately accountable helped. It could be to shareholders, teammates, family members or even yourself. Shifting focus and energy away from your relationship with a toxic leader and onto your primary responsibilities is something that you can control and it will help manage the relationship.

I also made sure that communication and contact were at the minimum. Nothing was withheld, of course, but no information was given that was not required. I often find that with poor leaders, the more information you provide, the more they use it either against you or to assign additional unnecessary work.

On occasion, you'll need to run interference on behalf of your team and protect them from a toxic boss. This is important because, as you recall, you have a responsibility to ensure that you create an environment that facilitates optimum performance for everyone. Being your best self sometimes means being and doing what's best for others.

Let's understand that a poor relationship with any leader you need to interact with, including family and friends, is not healthy or optimum for anyone; sometimes we need to adjust to bypass an obstacle that's preventing us from being our best. Has anyone been an obstacle for you? How did you handle it? How would you handle it now?

I once gave away my right to do the appropriate thing as the result of an emotional reaction, and it's one of my greatest regrets. Two going away events were usually held when senior members of Standard Life retired. One was a private dinner with a few very close colleagues, and one was a late-afternoon cocktail that anyone in the company was welcome to attend. When it was my turn to retire, our policy changed, as dictated by our UK office. A small budget was allocated for one event only. We had approximately 1500 employees in our head office at the time and I found the budget insulting. I asked Human Resources to take the budget and spend it on our staff and decided not to participate in any retirement event. My senior vice presidents appealed to me and even lobbied my wife to convince me otherwise, but my mind was made. My final *Online with Joseph* newsletter would be my farewell address. It was difficult and emotional writing it because, as much as I loved Standard Life, I loved our people more. To this day, when asked what I miss most about Standard Life, I always respond with "our people." In retrospect, not having the opportunity to personally say goodbye, shake hands and hug everyone is a regret. I was upset that our policy changed, and I let my emotions get the best of me. This is not the sign of a good boss. My executive team did surprise me with a cocktail event in our boardroom that was very much appreciated. My retirement gift from them? A set of beautiful racing rims and tires for my Fiat 500. Best retirement gift ever!

From CEO to Actor

Soon after formally retiring from the corporate world, I decided to give acting a try as a hobby. Predictably, I went in full throttle, enrolling in acting lessons and applying for auditions as soon as possible. I began to obtain some small roles and had a lot of fun. It wasn't going to end there, so I began to take it more seriously and eventually was fortunate enough to gain the lead male role in a low-budget indie film called *Crimson Sands*. The story was good, and I became a coproducer. The film won numerous international awards, but the journey certainly wasn't easy.

I knew nothing about producing a film, and as a result, the learning curve was steep. As a producer, you need to be hands-on to make sure things are aligned properly and move forward on a timely basis. Delays cost money, and our production didn't have much of it. My greatest challenge was not the technical details of the production, or the stress of acting itself, it was a combination of everything. Life on a film set can be tense. Everyone is under pressure to stay within budget and perform at their best, but the strain affects everyone differently. Stress can cause a lot of friction if it's not managed properly. We filmed for nineteen of twenty-three days allocated for production, sometimes traveling to different locations during the same day. Our personal lives were put on hold. That didn't help.

Despite all of this, the cast and crew were committed to being their best under the circumstances. It was important because we were determined to create the best film that we could. I too had a responsibility to the cast and crew to give my best effort. This is a perfect example of how you need to focus on being your best self to achieve the best possible result.

Beware of the Bullshit Artist

I cannot stress enough how important it is to be on the lookout for people who think and speak as if they're experts in everything but actually know extraordinarily little at best. They are indeed artists, and some are exceptionally talented. Some of them are so eloquent and smooth that it doesn't seem as if they're speaking Manurese, at first. Yes, Manurese is a language. It sounds like English, but it's a special dialect rooted in manure. When we don't really pay attention, it doesn't sound like nonsense, but eventually, it always does. Sometimes they end up in leadership positions.

These people are antagonists within an organization and your life and don't last long in either. That's because they're usually exposed and move from company to company, friend to friend and partner to partner. You can never fully trust what they say or be confident that they'll follow through on their commitments. Nothing ever seems to be their fault, and they always have an excuse for poor performance.

They can appear quite knowledgeable as they can articulate their viewpoint clearly. These people usually take a little bit of information on a topic and try to convince their audience that they have an encyclopedic knowledge of it, especially if their audience is not knowledgeable about what they're referring to. Their verbal diarrhea is impressive. They typically interview very well for jobs and make good first impressions. If you suspect that you have encountered one, leave. Just leave. If you want to confirm your suspicion or just have some fun, keep listening to them. They love to talk and talk and talk. They always give themselves away eventually. Once you get over how annoying they are, you'll find them amusing and entertaining. They'll never help you to achieve greatness.

If you need to tell the world that you're smart, successful, honest and all that, you more than likely aren't.

I Didn't See That One Coming

Fortunately, most of the people I hired throughout my career turned out to be great additions to our teams. However, not all have been successful. It's important to address the situation as soon as you realize you've made an error. I spoke to someone who I was convinced would be an asset to our organization. The person was one of those people who interview extremely well, skillfully embellish their achievements, but just don't live up to the billing. In addition to me, two others interviewed this person. All provided excellent feedback and rave reviews. After a few months, I knew I'd made a mistake and needed to perform one of the most difficult tasks a manager is required to do, relieve someone of their duties. This person was someone I just didn't have a good read on as to how they'd react to the news. It could go any number of ways. Human Resources prepared all of the paperwork, and the time and date were set for our meeting. The evening before breaking the news, I visualized several different scenarios, thinking about what to say and how to say it. Within each of these scenarios, I envisioned how the person could react and how I'd respond. This went on for some time. I finally felt comfortable that, no matter what happened, I had been there before in my mind and would be able to handle it. Of course, none of the scenarios that were visualized actually materialized. The person understood the rationale, was pleasant and professional. I recall they were somewhat relieved. We both realized that the fit with the company wasn't good and that we needed to move on. Despite all my preparation and anticipation of what might unfold, the person fooled me again! Their reaction was the last thing I expected.

Beware of the Arsonist and Firefighter

The universe provides each of us with an incredible amount of abundance of which we're all deserving. There are some who don't realize this and need to generate their own perception of importance, hoping it will lead to rewards. These are the types of people who create a fire then swoop in as the firefighter and savior. These are bad leaders.

This is different than when someone makes an error and quickly mobilizes to fix it. The arsonist and firefighter purposely sets a fire and creates a situation that can be dangerous or is perceived to be. They then offer solutions to solve the crisis and emerge as heroes. Politicians are notorious for using this strategy to secure voter support. Some executives that suspect their jobs are in danger will try it as a desperate attempt to save their jobs and demonstrate their ability to navigate through a crisis.

Conversely, good leaders can use this same strategy for productive reasons. Sometimes one needs to light a small fire somewhere in order to temporarily take people's minds off of something. This type of distraction will help steer their focus away from something negative toward something positive. I've used it on occasion to create a diversion from an unpleasant situation at work or at home. I recall distracting my son from an upset stomach when he was about six years old. After determining that his condition was not serious, I suggested playing a video game on my laptop, something that he wasn't allowed to do often. Almost immediately, the pain was manageable.

Never Micromanage

I'm convinced that the absolute worst thing that a leader can do is to micromanage their people. I've seen too many leaders put together a strong team, only to limit their ability to be their best by suppressing their talents and placing creative shackles on them. It's better to have to rein someone in than constantly motivate them. It's exhausting and counterproductive. Micromanaging "thoroughbreds" never turns out well as they'll be frustrated and eventually leave. Give them responsibilities that they can handle, support them, and let them run. Be their safety net, but let them try to jump the high hurdles. They have the company's best interests in mind as well as yours.

It's easy to micromanage, especially for new leaders or leaders that have been promoted within their departments. They know their old job well and expect someone to do it in the same manner as they did, not acknowledging the uniqueness of the new person. Also, new leaders sometimes want to focus on the work of their employees because they believe, understandably, that their work is a reflection of their own performance. They want the work to be perfect, and the only way that it can be is if they're involved in every aspect of it because they want to justify the confidence that management has given them. Unfortunately, this has the opposite effect. It stifles productivity and creativity and creates a stressful environment for everyone. The employees are stressed because it seems that everything they do is monitored in fine detail, and the manager is stressed because it takes a great deal of energy to micro-manage. Ironically, when a leader micromanages, they're taking time away from what they should actually be doing—coaching people to be their best. There are countless courses, books and seminars on how to effectively manage people. None of them include micromanaging. A micromanager doesn't seem to understand or accept that members of their team most likely know much more about the details of their specific jobs than the manager does.

In my experience, the most effective manner in which to be successful and achieve everything that you want is to put a team in place and give them the space and resources necessary to do their jobs. My approach was simple. I'd outline what we wanted to accomplish as our end goal and have everyone figure out their own way to get there. My responsibility was to be supportive at all times and to help everyone be happy and at their best.

Besides our corporate scorecard, which we produced each month as the primary strategic plan monitoring report, I left it up to my team to inform me of activities within their departments. Initially, they'd ask what I wanted to know. My response usually was, "Tell me what you think I should know. Just make sure that there are no surprises." In all of my years in leadership in a corporate environment, I was always kept up to date on the goings-on of our company and was rarely surprised, if ever. Micromanaging would have resulted in getting much "too deep in the weeds" and being inundated with useless information.

Strive to be the leader that you'd want to work for and trust your team.

Destructive Coaching

In the late 1980s, I worked as a salesperson in the Toronto Group Life and Health office of Standard Life and was fortunate enough to be doing well. A new manager was hired a few months after my hiring, and from the beginning, he'd ask me about the day's sales activities, about follow-ups on renewals, broker calls, and so on. I'd provide him with daily updates, but it didn't end there, he proceeded to tell me how to craft letters and draft emails. He basically felt the need to tell me how to do my job, a job that I was successful at already. I knew my customers and brokers well and knew how to best influence their behavior. I was open to ideas that would help with productivity, of course. After all, most of my compensation was variable and based on sales, and if someone could help me sell more, I was grateful for it. However, this wasn't constructive coaching; it was micromanaging, and it was non-productive. It was destructive coaching, something that discourages strong performance and diminishes your ability to succeed. It needed to stop. One day, when I was in his office going through the daily micromanage routine, I stopped him in midsentence and suggested that he must think that I had a memory problem. He asked why I'd think that. I said, "Because you must think that I need to be trained every day for things that I've been doing effectively for my entire sales career. I know how to do my job and will keep you informed of what's important." He was slightly taken aback, but to his credit, he stepped back and provided space for me to continue to focus on my responsibilities. Sometimes calling out someone who is micromanaging is the right thing to do. This can help them realize what they're doing is not helpful to being at their best nor is it helping you achieve what you're capable of.

During your life and career, you'll encounter many different types of leaders, some good ones and some bad ones. If you can't find a way to work with a poor leader by outsmarting them or adopting another strategy that works for you, move away from them as soon as feasibly possible, even if you love your job. On the other hand, if you can adapt and still manage to grow and thrive, do so while you can, but understand that their negative energy will eventually have a destructive effect on your performance.

Let's take a look again at the list at the beginning of this chapter and reconsider all of the similar traits that bad leaders share. Each of these traits is a Diminishing Effect. Some of them may apply to people you know. Striving to be your best can appear to be a daunting task at times—the last thing you need is a poor leader who undermines your efforts.

Now ask yourself, "Do any of those traits apply to me?" If so, write them down.

_____

_____

_____

_____

_____

_____

If your list is blank, great! If not, what will you do to make sure that you don't have a Diminishing Effect on yourself or others?

CHAPTER 13

Structurally Sound

Ahhh, perfection! Can you imagine? As good as can be, impossible to improve. It is done and concluded because it is perfect. Such a finite definition—for an inanimate object. What about a living being? What is perfection in this case?

We are taught to believe that a perfect human being doesn't exist, that no one is perfect, but I disagree. I believe that being perfect has as many definitions as the number of humans on earth. We all have our personal definition of what perfection is within ourselves, all living things as well as all inanimate objects. We define what is perfect for us.

This is why, to become your best self, you must understand your unique definition of what perfection is. Becoming your best self means becoming your own definition of perfection. There's no settling here—we exist to be as good as can be. And because we're dynamic beings that are ever-changing within ever-changing surroundings, we need to live and create structures within our environment that accommodate our path to personal growth and perfection. Let's be clear, there will be some failure along the way. But only you can decide whether failure is fatal or whether it's an opportunity to learn and grow as you journey through the wonders of life.

The Multiplier Effect of Structure

When you think of structure, you may think of something static, but structure, using a very general definition, is simply something that's the end result of putting many parts together. This could mean a physical structure, like our bodies or a concrete building, but it can also be something that's nonphysical in nature. It can be dynamic, elastic and flowing; it can be able to constantly change. Understanding how to create a structure that facilitates a clear path to enrichment, in every area of your personal and professional life, is important in achieving your best self. Understanding when to adapt and change structures is equally important.

The Importance of Family Structure

Families are structural units that need to work together well if they're going to thrive. This is especially true for the immediate family, but also for any relationship where there is a sharing of a household.

When our first child was born, like most parents, we had to rely on intuition to care for a newborn, navigating through available information and unsolicited advice. We naturally settled on doing what each of us is comfortable with and it worked out fine. Mary and I have always worked together to determine what works best for our family unit. As an example, after some experimentation and a little confusion early on in our marriage, we figured out some basic guidelines for how responsibilities should be shared. There are many things that need to be done to run a smooth household, and clearly defined roles for each member work best. It should be noted that, for us, some of these general guidelines naturally developed over time, and some were purposefully discussed. There is little confusion or overlap, and we're always each other's backup. We based our shared responsibilities on our strengths and what we do best. It was as simple as that. We didn't consider traditional male and female roles.

Mary loves to cook and can make incredible dishes from various countries and cultures. She's incredibly good and is always trying new recipes. Naturally, Mary does most of the cooking in our family. I consider myself handy and am especially passionate about different types of tools, cars and gardening. Besides fixing things around the house, it's my responsibility to keep our vehicles in good working order and make sure that our landscaping isn't an embarrassment to the neighborhood. If Mary tells me that there's something wrong with her car or that she needs basil for her pesto recipe, I'm on it. This applies even when we do things together. If we decide to paint a room, Mary is responsible for all door trim, baseboard taping and any other areas that require finesse because she has the patient, steady hand. I handle the main walls and ceiling. This clear separation of responsibilities applies to most things in our household, and it works extremely well. If something new or unexpected comes up that needs to be done, and neither of us is motivated to do it, our tiebreaker question is, "Who is best suited to do it?" Then Mary, with a cunning instinct and a keen awareness of my ego, somehow convinces me that I'm so much better suited than she is to take on the new task. She's a great negotiator!

Clearly defined roles and responsibilities are especially important if anything is going to run smoothly within an optimum structure. Confusion, uncertainty or overlapping responsibilities usually leads to frustration. You should clearly understand your role whether within yourself or your family, your workplace or society. You should also clearly understand your role in the world and the universe and how it affects other beings.

Corporate Structure

An Appropriate for Now structure within an organization will foster an environment for accelerated growth for the organization and all of its employees. When robust, it will align with the strategic plan and offer opportunities for employees to grow, be their best, contribute to positive results and be rewarded appropriately. There will be no pain points or obstacles to stifle growth. Communication will flow freely, products and services will be produced on a timely basis, everyone will be supported, and the company will flourish.

Corporate leaders should always build their teams and corporate structure in alignment with the business plan, not the other way around. Each year, once our strategic plan was approved by our Canadian and UK board of directors, we examined our corporate structure to ensure that it was the right one to achieve our strategic objectives. Once we were convinced that the structure was optimal to our success, we reassessed our talent to make sure they had the appropriate skills to execute our plan. If not, we adjusted by reassigning roles and responsibilities. I made two major corporate structural changes during my seven years as CEO of Standard Life of Canada. We'd just created a comprehensive strategy that was bold and aggressive. It focused on playing to our strengths and making certain that our weaknesses didn't hurt us. We then thought about the corporate structure that would be required to implement our plan successfully and our team created an organizational chart that made sense. Once we did this, we filled in the names of our talent that would be ideal in the roles we created. Once done, we were left with a list of people who were not assigned roles. The people who we believed could contribute to our success were retained with roles within their areas of expertise, while others were assigned stretch roles that we believed they would be successful in. It was rare that we let people go, but when it was required, we always treated them fairly and wished them well.

Great organizations and leaders create corporate structures, cultures and environments that are appropriate for what they want to accomplish at that particular time. They are unique to each company and need to be created as such. Reading a book, attending a seminar or adopting someone else's structure will not necessarily make your organization successful.

Different Strokes for Different Folks

The propensity for working remotely, often from our homes, has no doubt influenced how companies look at their structure to optimise their performance while making their employees happy. People, and their personal preference for working in an office or at home, will influence how new working models evolve.

There are many reasons why companies change from one structure to another. It could be to adapt to a new way of working due to an unexpected event, like a pandemic. It could also be to accommodate a new strategic direction or to facilitate the implementation of a new strategy. It could be an attempt at reorganization to appease shareholders if the company is not performing well. Corporate structures are also usually changed as a result of mergers or acquisitions.

The primary concept to understand is that only internal leaders can determine what's best for your organization. If you're a leader, you should have a keen awareness of what's needed to achieve your objectives. The corporate structure is important because it helps determine what happens within the organization. Good companies develop an Appropriate for Now structure that allows people within it to be their best.

Good companies understand that it's ultimately the people within the organization that will be the primary driver for the attainment of their goals, not the structure, although it is very important. This is something we discussed in Chapters 9 and 10. Therefore, if you have an opinion as to how to make a change within the structure of your organization to improve your chances of being your best, bring it to the attention of anyone that can help. Good leaders understand that a solid structure should set the stage for overall prosperity. A good leader will consider reporting lines and communication channels, define clear responsibilities and promote ease of creativity and innovation. Strong governance and accountability are also essential. All of these need to be considered to ensure everyone has an opportunity to contribute to the best of their abilities. However, they don't always know what will work for everyone. If you have an idea, it's important to share it.

As a youth and well into my early corporate years, I read as many self-help and self-improvement books as possible. These included all kinds of different categories, including ones explaining dream interpretation, body language, leadership styles, personal relationships and emotional intelligence. I admired people who were successful and desired to emulate them.

Autobiographies and leadership books written by very popular and successful leaders of great companies were a favorite. I admired their success, accumulation of wealth, power, popularity and influence. On occasion, something useful would resonate that applied to my personal situation. These hundreds of hours of reading helped me realize that most of the information provided was either common sense or updated ancient wisdom from different cultures. Not much of the information was new; it was "dusted off and repackaged." I understood that you shouldn't necessarily do what others have done, you should learn from what they've experienced, elevate their ideas to a higher level and use them if they apply to you. Always consider the source of the information and trust your decision-making process to do what's right for you. Keep in mind that if you gather too much information or advice, especially in quick succession, you'll do nothing more than confuse yourself. It is best to stay away from what I refer to as flavor-of-the-day solutions. There will always be someone suggesting what's best for you. Do what you believe is best for you.

Make Changes for the Better

Just because something is not broken, it doesn't mean that it shouldn't be fixed. Remember the Appropriate for Now concept? Something can be working very well for what you want to accomplish at the moment, but not for the future. Don't be loyal to old structures even if they have served you well in the past. They've done just that, served you well for what existed in the past, but if they won't serve you well into the future, make changes before you're forced to by unforeseen circumstances. This applies in both personal and professional life.

We're often too late in realizing that something is broken, we're then forced to change for the better or live and die with the consequences. Sometimes we refuse to accept that circumstances are changing and that a shift of some sort is required to continue moving forward. Let's think about this for a minute. Do you remember an instance where you needed or were forced to make a significant change in your life? This could be a job, relationship, career or where to live. Did you procrastinate? Did you avoid making the change because things were okay? How about the ever-reliable excuse of hoping that someone or some change in circumstance would make the decision for you? Postponement or avoidance isn't productive. Change is difficult. We know that. Changing the structure of a company, personal circumstances, or a relationship is one of the most stressful things that we need to consider in everyday life if we want to achieve our best selves. I've coached many people who've been reluctant to change, mostly because of fear of failure or fear of the unknown.

The year after we made record revenue and profits at Standard Life, we implemented a significant corporate structural change. I personally believed that the structure we had in place was useful for facilitating our past objectives. We were now ready to enter into a period of aggressive growth with a new strategy, and we needed a new structure, with an investment in technology, to underpin it. We needed to be nimbler as an organization, facilitate innovation and creativity, open up opportunities for emerging talent and reduce internal bureaucracy for new product and service launches. As you can imagine, this decision wasn't taken lightly. The thinking was understood and supported by our chairperson, but our executive team required more convincing. Most didn't see the benefits of implementing a significant, time-consuming and disruptive change at that particular time. The competition and competitive environment were moving fast, and we needed to keep up our momentum. Our strategy at that time was to be a "fast follower" for most innovations, and I wanted us to lead, especially in areas that we considered our strengths and in which we had a market advantage. We made the changes, and the company continued to grow.

The path toward being your best self is not linear. There will be times when you need to decide among different avenues. You know that you'll eventually move forward, but one route may offer a short-cut over another. This sometimes happens at a point of inflection and applies to everyday life, whether personal or professional. There will be times when your life is well-balanced and comfortable. Don't consider this a sign that you can be complacent. It may be the best time for a change for the (much) better.

Let's contemplate an example in your personal life. Let's say that you're deep into a relationship that has plateaued. If so, the nature and structure of the relationship need to be looked at if it's going to continue to thrive, even if it's comfortable. If not, there will be a realization that something is wrong, and you'll be forced to change the dynamic. If you're truly committed, you'll come to this realization, make changes and emerge stronger within the relationship. If not, you'll go through a cycle of happy and unhappy periods, ultimately resulting in a slow decline of the relationship. This applies to all of us. People change as they move through their life stages. Let's not be satisfied with being in a good relationship. We should strive to make every relationship great by embracing opportunities for positive changes.

Overall Success

Each year at Standard Life my chief financial officer and I conducted what we called the President's Tour. We visited each office across Canada to present our year-end results and our business plan for the following year. Christian handled the financials, and I took care of the strategy. To break the monotony of presenting for several hours straight, I'd speak to the audience for fifteen minutes or so in between presentations. We had a different theme each year.

One year, I wanted to convey the message that everyone's role is critical to the overall success of the company within our structure. Sometimes this is difficult to see if you view your role as limited in scope and importance. This is absolutely not true. We're all linked to each other.

I invited an audience member onstage and asked these questions:

Me: What do you do at Standard Life?

Member: I work in IT.
Me: What do you do in IT?

Member: I'm working on our new pension administration system project.

Me: Who needs to do their job well in order for you to do yours well? At this point, most mentioned their bosses, or if they were managing people, their team. This is excellent and completely understandable but not where I was going with the exercise.

Me: Who else needs to do their job well so that you can do yours well? This usually prompted a little more thought.

Member: My boss's boss?

Me: Of course. Who else?

Sometimes they'd get stuck here and required some prompting.

Me: How about the people in Human Resources?

A puzzled look followed.

Me: Does Human Resources need to do their job well so that you can do yours well? Do they need to study and understand salary scales, do they need to pay you on time and accurately, arrange proper training for you and administer your benefits? Do you reach out to them when you need to hire a new person or are looking to find another challenge within our company?

Member: Of course!

Me: Who else? How about Finance? Do they need to manage the finances of the company properly so that we can continue to grow and afford the project that you're working on?

Member: Of course!

Me: How about our Sales division? Do they need to achieve their sales targets in order for Finance to manage the money so we can have enough to fund the project that you're working on?

Member: Of course!

By this time, all understood where I was headed in my messaging. Everyone, from our amazing custodians to our board of directors, had an important common link to our success, and each was an essential piece of our structure. If we observe correctly, everyone's job is related to everyone else's, and we need everyone to be at their best to succeed.

This story is symbolic of every role that we play within society. We should understand that we have an important part to play in the success of the universe. We're interconnected, and we're all as one within the universal structure. Nature will be in complete balance and harmony if we understand that by being 100 percent our best selves, we're helping all living things become as such. This is why we need to do everything at 100 percent. If we don't, we're depriving others of the chance to be their best because everything we do is linked to everything and everyone else in some way.

The obvious is merely something that conceals what is truly accessible.

Creativity Turned On

At Standard Life we wanted our organization to be more creative in product development and services for our customers and considered this whenever we modified our corporate structure. The insurance industry is not generally known for its dynamic and innovative culture. It could be if it realized just how capable its employees are of being incredibly creative and innovative. Everyone is naturally creative as a child, but as they get older, they get held back by rules, culture, guidelines and yes, structures. To remind people that they're all capable of developing original and inspired ideas, I conducted an exercise during a meeting with approximately four hundred Standard Life employees.

I stood in front of them with a prop. The prop could be literally anything. I used a pen in this particular case. I held it up and asked, "What is this?" Of course, it's a pen, and everyone responded as such. The fun started when I asked what else it could be.

These were some examples out of the thirty-two the employees came up with.

"A weapon."

"A doorstop."

"A hair tie."

"A measuring stick."

"A rocket."

"A hole puncher."

The creativity was stunning. We performed this exercise a few times using different props. It was great fun and awe-inspiring to see what everyone came up with. Everyone understood that their inherent creativity was still buried within them and that it just needed to come closer to the surface. They returned to their desks with a newfound appreciation of what's possible within the structure of their environment. Simply by using their imaginations and unleashing their inner child, they were ready to create new products and services for our customers.

I've mentioned several times that people are the most important resources that will drive success. Great people make up for a lot of bad things. Once you have a process for hiring excellent people, whether you're in a position of leadership or not, it's your responsibility to create an environment with conditions that facilitate everyone being their best possible selves. To this end, an important element in your professional and personal life is how you have structured it to best suit your needs.

Imagine a structure as a river. Now, imagine kayaking in the river. Your goal is to arrive at a specific destination. If the river is cluttered with fallen logs, rocks and other obstacles, your journey will likely be treacherous, time-consuming and energy-sapping. You will need to navigate among the many obstacles to arrive at your ultimate destination. In contrast, if the river is free-flowing with few barriers or stumbling blocks, you would arrive sooner, you would enjoy the surroundings more and be more refreshed upon arrival.

The universe is a series of structures, and you need to find the ones that serve as Multiplier Effects for your success. These are the types of structures that don't have obstacles blocking you from getting where you ultimately want to be. Only you can determine which ones work best for you.

CHAPTER 14

Being Present

There are times when being present is absolutely necessary. You should have an acute awareness of what's happening at that very instant.

Being in the moment, without judgment, helps you experience life to its fullest. This helps you become the best you can be and realize the effect you can then have on others. Being focused on what's happening within you at any given moment, with no consideration of past and future, helps you observe and learn. You'll appreciate the world around you because you'll understand how you're woven into it. Within your mind, you can be anything, anywhere and anyone at any time. There are absolutely no rules or limitations unless you impose them on yourself. Your mind can wander off to wherever you guide it. It can choose its own setting—past, present or future. You can imagine telling a joke to friends and laughing out loud or you can imagine debating how to resolve a problem with two or three versions of yourself. There are absolutely no boundaries. What happens in your mind is your business, and this is a wonderful thing.

Your body, on the other hand, doesn't have this kind of freedom and must be somewhere, in the present time, always. Your physical body cannot be anywhere else but where it is right now.

Therefore, naturally, there can be a disconnect between where your mind and body are. It seems that, in today's world, the two are rarely in the same place at the same time. This is often viewed as a negative thing. Yogis focus on being present throughout their practice. Bringing attention to their breath and what's happening in their bodies as they move through the asanas is important. If I catch myself wandering off during yoga practice, I quickly refocus on my breath and bring myself back to what's happening in that moment. During yoga teacher training, I was constantly reminded to be "in the moment" at all times and was taught that we'll miss something if we're not always present, but I believe that on occasion it is perfectly fine to purposely choose not to be totally present. I understand the difficulty of being present at all times, especially in our busy world. There are always multiple things to think of simultaneously. This is fine, as long as you decide when you are to be present and realize that it should be most of the time and that it's necessary to be your best self.

> *It's your responsibility to acknowledge the past, live in the present and imagine the future.*

Sometimes, not being present can help us cope with all kinds of situations, some of which are unpleasant or unfavorable. Let me share a personal example. I was completely present in the moment at the funeral home when an aunt passed. There were beautiful flowers all around, family and friends talking, and my aunt's face looked peaceful. Looking at her, my mind explored the past and recalled several good times I enjoyed with her, including a holiday dinner and one of her jokes that made me laugh again. Then my mind jumped to the future and wondered what kinds of conversations she'd have with my father now that they could catch up in the afterlife. Sometimes, being present is of no consequence. You need to have enough control to make sure that you're present when required to be so. Another example of the importance of being present is when your full concentration is required to successfully complete a task, like writing an important exam or learning to drive. If you're focused on a specific task, your conscious mind is active in helping you concentrate and focus on what needs to be done. If you're in the middle of performing such a task and your mind wanders off elsewhere, your subconscious mind is activated, and whatever it has been programmed to do will determine the result of the task at hand and there can be consequences. Let me explain. Have you ever caught yourself driving home, as you've done countless times, only to miss your exit, reawaken to your conscious state and wonder, how did I get here? Have you ever read a chapter in a book only to have to read and re-read it many times before you comprehend it? This happens not because you don't understand the concept, but because your mind is elsewhere while you continue to actively read the words. I've done this many times. If you're doing it now, catch yourself and come back!

Being in and out of the present state is natural. Understanding and controlling when this happens is important and a part of the growing process of being your best self.

> *If I enter your life or you enter mine unexpectedly, it is not a coincidence. We have been brought together for a reason. Just accept and let the reason reveal itself. It will become clear.*

Wake Up to Wisdom

When I was promoted to vice president, my job transferred to Montreal. Mary and I decided to keep the kids in school for the year, enjoy the summer in Toronto and then move as a family in the fall. That meant that I'd commute to Montreal weekly for approximately eight months.

The flight schedule was the same each week. As a matter of fact, there were others who had the same schedule. I'd see them each Tuesday morning on the six thirty a.m. flight and quite often on the Friday night flight home.

I hated leaving my family each week. I really did. The thought of leaving my wife and three young children on their own and missing what they'd be doing upset me. Therefore, I made certain that I left the house before any of them woke up because I couldn't stand to say goodbye.

One morning, after several months of weekly traveling, Vincent, my middle son who was five at the time, was awake. He and Mary were on the couch as I was about to leave the house. Vincent looked up and asked, "Do you want to play cards, Dad?" I became very emotional and began to sob uncontrollably. Vincent was puzzled, but Mary understood. "Just go catch your plane. We'll be fine," she said. Mary called me just before my flight and asked whether I was okay. "No," was all I could say.

When I boarded the plane, an elderly gentleman that I'd seen almost every week on the same flight sat close by. We'd never spoken until then, but he must have sensed something by the look on my face and asked what was wrong. I'm not sure why, but I explained what had happened that morning. He said that he'd been commuting for a long time and that he'd experienced the same thing years before. "Leaving each week is difficult, for sure," he said. "I just made sure that when I was home, I was there, with my family, as part of their day and conversation. Your son won't remember you running errands, reading reports or watching television when you're home. He'll remember you teaching him how to ride a bike, how to tie his shoes, and helping him with his first shave. When you are home, be home. Don't be anywhere else." Then he went on to add, "Too many fathers are physically home and around their kids but pay no attention to them. They are still thinking about work or other things. Make sure that when you are home, you are creating memories." I've never forgotten those words.

Situational Friendships

It is a fact of life that some friendships are situational. We can become emotionally and physically attached to people because of a certain situational proximity. The relationship can naturally fade away once the reason people are together disappears. There is nothing wrong with this. When appropriate, we need to let go as we reflect on how we learned from it and how it helped us grow. We can look back on our experiences anytime.

Do any of the following situations sound familiar? Do any of them apply to you?

- Neighbors who are friends and lived on the same street or even next door to each other for many years don't have any contact at all after one of them moves.
- Inmates who are not gay but have same-sex affairs while in prison revert back to heterosexual activity when they are released.
- Actors working long hours on a set for days or months develop emotional ties, but the relationships end once the project ends.
- Co-workers who have worked closely together for many years have no further contact when one of them leaves.
- High school or university friends, who had strong relationships, completely lose contact when they graduate.

These are all examples of situational friendships, and you'll have many throughout your lifetime. If you're present during these relationships, you can look back and vividly experience them at any time.

I was one of thirty-two people enrolled in my yoga teacher training program. The course was intensive and delved into many aspects of our lives, including some personal. Vulnerability was encouraged, and we shared deep emotional experiences, both from past and present. We were crowded together in one room. We practiced together, assisted each other, ate together and basically shared almost everything. Many of us became very close. I reminded my fellow yogis to enjoy the moment because most of us would never see each other again. My friends countered with, "There is no way that will happen. We've shared so much and have become so close. We will stay in touch for sure." We even started a Facebook Group to remain in contact. Within a few weeks of the end of teacher training, everyone went back to their own lives, and we haven't seen each other since. Only yogis that practice or teach at the same studios see each other on occasion. The program kept us together, and once finished, so were most of our friendships. Situational friendships are what we had, and they were great, but brief.

People Will Love You, Until They Don't

Most relationships are self-serving. People will live and work together productively and happily as long as their own needs are fulfilled. Although this sounds negative, the relationship dynamics serves both parties. As soon as the dynamics change, positive or negative, the relationships change. Being in a relationship that serves all parties well causes a Multiplier Effect to occur.

Situational relationships, unlike true companions, are people who will be friendly as long as they perceive that they can benefit from you, and vice-versa. You may care for each other, but as soon as the dynamic changes, the relationship usually ends. One of the starkest examples of this occurred to my family and me when we lived in Montreal. Standard Life and a few other large companies were in high demand in terms of contributing to philanthropic activities. All major charities and capital campaigns lobby for contributions from these companies. We had an annual budget for corporate sponsorships, and we gifted to organizations that were aligned with our values and donation preferences. It was important to us that all of the major charity events were sponsored because they did such great work. Mary and I attended many important galas that took away from our family life but we did what we felt was our duty and responsibility to the community in which we lived and worked. The invitations stopped when I announced that I was retiring from Standard Life and moving back to Toronto. The community waited for my successor to be named to make sure that new commitments were secured. I had been present and had enjoyed the experiences, and it was now my replacement's turn.

People need a reason to be and stay together. Most often the reason is self-serving. When situations change, behaviors change as well. This is perfectly acceptable. We need to look upon situations as a time in our lives where we were brought together for a reason and that the relationships served their purpose for a period of time. This period could be brief or last many years. Be present, enjoy the moments, and move forward.

Curiosity Is Intelligence

What you know is finite. What you don't know is infinite. Try to approach each situation with curiosity, not intelligence. We don't know what we don't know, and each circumstance is a chance to learn something. I don't think about what I know or what views or opinions I have, nor do I think about the past or future. I'm present in each moment and have a completely open mind. By doing this, I understand that there are no boundaries imposed by what I've learned or what I know. My experience—what I've researched, or what someone has spoken to me about— serves as a limitation to how I behave during each circumstance.

Curiosity during a meeting or conversation allows you to be completely present and absorb all of the information that's presented before making decisions or comments. You can then take this information and process it through your internal filters of intelligence, experience and perception. You can now make conclusions and decisions that will affect the future, but you'll have made them with consideration of only what is present. If you approach something with what you know or understand—hence, a reflection of your past, mostly memory, learning and experience—you risk imposing unnecessary limitations to your ability to make independent and objective comments and decisions. Have you ever been in a conversation where you formulated a response in your mind while the person was still talking?

Learn to be present and listen intently. Be humble enough to realize that the person or people you're listening to have something to say that's important and that you'll learn something new from them.

Strong listening skills don't just apply to people. Listen intently, always. This includes every sound that you hear. You'll be surprised at what you'll learn.

Let's consider an example. As you're reading this, what sounds do you hear in the background? Music? Perhaps a chair squeaking or the humming of an appliance at work. Listen intently to whatever sounds are present. What can you learn from these sounds? If your focus is intense and you're present in the moment, the possibilities to learn are enormous. The lyrics of a song could be a learning experience as could imagining the origin of the squeaking noise of a chair. There's something to take away from every sound that we hear.

Being present is magic, and the wonderful thing is that you decide when to be so. It's when your physical body and mind are in the same place at the same time; enjoying the moment is being at ease and comfortable with what's happening within and around you. With complete and clear awareness, you can enjoy every detail of your immediate existence. This allows for a maximum learning experience within each moment and is a powerful Multiplier Effect.

CHAPTER 15

Focus Your Energy and Trust the Process

The Potential to Lose Focus

Since my father's passing, I'm responsible for looking after my mom as I am an only child. While living in Montreal, I was on my way to a convention center to deliver a speech. It was my first significant speech in front of over two hundred colleagues and associates, and I was nervous. While I was in the car, my mom called. "The furnace is not working. I'm cold." It was in the middle of winter on a weekday evening. "Did you ask Cleo next door to look at it?" Cleo was a fantastic neighbor and a great human being. He was my go-to person if my mom needed something looked at. "Yes, and he said that it's broken." I was on my way to the most important speech of my career, and my mom calls because her furnace is broken. I'm in Montreal, and she's at home in Toronto. Talk about the potential to lose focus! "Give me a few minutes, and I'll call you back." A quick call to Louie, someone who'd done some furnace work for us before, solved the problem. Louie promised that it'd be taken care of. I let my mom know that he was on his way. I arrived at the convention center ready to refocus on my speech. Half an hour later, Mom called again. "There is someone outside that wants to speak to you." She handed the phone to someone. "Hi, Joseph. This is Paul, Louie's brother. He sent me to take care of your mom, but she won't let me in without your consent." I politely asked Paul to let me speak to my mom again. "*Let him in!*" I think Paul must have heard me from where he was standing outside. She let him in, and I asked why in the world she'd call me again once help arrived. She calmly replied, "You said that Louie would come to fix the furnace, and he's not Louie. Why would I let a stranger in my home?" That's my mom. Not long after my mom's second call, I was introduced to deliver my speech. I didn't let the distraction affect my ability to perform and was laser-focused on the content, pause points, hand gestures and audience feedback. Don't allow distractions to steer your attention away from your goal.

> *If our minds are too focused on the future, we perform poorly in the present. We should focus on the process and the outcome we desire will occur naturally.*

Focused Energy as a Multiplier for Success

As humans, we have an enormous amount of physical and emotional energy available to us. The problem for most of us is that we simultaneously disperse it in too many different directions. We think of multiple things at the same time. We're constantly thinking about and doing things simultaneously, often bragging about being "great multi-taskers." I used to think in this manner, but soon realized that it's not conducive to being your best self at all times. I often like to use the analogy of a river. The narrower and more focused it is, the more powerful. The energy of our minds and thoughts works in the same manner. If we think about too many things simultaneously, we won't give enough attention to what matters most at that time. If we're not present and don't give 100 percent energy and attention to the most important task at hand, we'll be disappointed with the results. The Multiplier Effect, in this instance, is to focus your thoughts and actions on what will aid you in optimally performing the task at hand. I know it seems easier said than done in this world. I invite you to experiment and focus on one task at a time for one day. If this is too difficult, perhaps start with prioritizing tasks and work your way down the list, focussing on one at a time. If you don't accomplish everything, no worries. The most important ones will be taken care of. You may be surprised with the results.

What do we naturally find time to intently focus our attention on? Activities and subjects that we are passionate about. These are always a true indicator of what will make you happiest during your journey to your best self. We all know of people who eat, live and breathe a particular activity. It's all they think about and they have unlimited amounts of energy to expend toward it. If you find an element of passion in your job, your chores or any process, you'll perform better. This is key to becoming your best self. I'm passionate about yoga and helping others. What are you passionate about?

Sometimes You Need Multiple Lines to Catch a Fish

In 1999, our Group Life and Health division was losing $29 million per year on a book of business (revenue base) of approximately $220 million. We don't need to be mathematical geniuses to understand that this isn't a good scenario. I was Vice-President, and our president gave my team three years to make the division profitable.

Pierre was an extremely talented actuary that headed our pricing division for Group Life and Health. Our opposite characteristics and skills complemented each other very well.

Pierre and I thought long and hard as to what we could do to start making profits while also growing the portfolio. Generally, growing rapidly and turning a profit in the insurance industry are diametrically opposed. To rapidly grow a portfolio, a company usually reduces its prices. Cheaper pricing will result in greater sales but will hamper profitability. An increase in pricing will move a portfolio closer to profitability but will reduce the size of revenues because customers will take their business elsewhere. We needed to somehow develop a strategy that would accomplish both objectives. Because it was too risky and the cost of failure was too high, we didn't consider a "hit a home run" approach whereby we'd make two or three radical adjustments and hope one of them would work. We decided to use the "throw everything at the wall and see what sticks" approach instead. We implemented thirty-two different initiatives, some that had small incremental effects and some that we expected would be more impactful. We even isolated long-term accounts that were chronically money-losing for us and issued an ultimatum to the consultants representing them—either they could work with us to stop the bleeding, or they could take their business elsewhere. Kill or Cure, remember? This is a great example. We knew that each of the initiatives would have various degrees of success, but as a collective, if we focused on our goal and implemented enough of them, the results would be powerful. We just needed to let them run their course and be patient. It was the right approach, the results were outstanding. We turned a profit within two years, and the business continued to grow profitably thereafter.

Play to Win

Understand and mitigate risk, but always take a risk. You can't become your best self if you avoid risks and don't take chances in life. I consider myself a risk-taker, but my approach is to not take foolish risks or chance something that's not well thought through. Simply understand the risks and develop a plan to mitigate them. As an example, when engaging in a competition, concentrate on studying the landscape and practice as much as possible to enhance your chances for success. Personally, for most things, I participate only if there's a reasonable chance of success, and then, with laser focus, I play to win. If successful, great, and if not, there's comfort in knowing that I more than likely learned something and did what was possible to achieve the desired result. For me, the only exception to this rule is playing the lottery. I'll purchase a ticket once in a while for fun and clearly understand that the risk of failure is astronomical. But hey, if the jackpot is large enough, someone has to win.

People take risks on others all of the time. Throughout my career, I was fortunate that people took many chances with me and provided me with opportunities for growth and advancement. My not having prior experience for a new role didn't dissuade them. This may also have happened to you, or you may have taken a chance on someone you believed in. A couple of examples could be a mechanic hiring a young apprentice or a manager having faith in a young athlete to play in an important game. Sometimes people take chances on themselves. A great example of this is Fred VanVleet, a professional basketball player. Fred knew that he had the ability to become a professional basketball player despite being bypassed by every team on draft day. He signed a minor deal with Toronto and simply focused his attention on improving. He reduced his chances of failure by practicing and working hard, studying opponents and continuing to learn the game of basketball. He has complete self-awareness of who he is and what he's capable of. Fred began his career in the developmental league, worked his way up to the Toronto Raptors and played a significant role in winning a championship. His tagline, Bet on Yourself, suits him perfectly.

Why Me?

I was thrilled when told that I had been appointed as Sales Manager of Standard Life's Group Life and Health office. Appreciative of the opportunity, I asked Doug why he hired me as I had never managed anything prior. Doug explained that the risk was minimal in his view because he had confidence in my ability to meet the expectations for the job. Besides, he would do his best to help me succeed. It's a simple enough answer, but I now know what he meant because I've experienced the same when asking people to take on responsibilities that are new.

Yes, I believe that I took a risk on them, but from my perspective, the risk associated with the decision was minimal and mitigated. I believed they would perform well within their new responsibilities and was willing to support them to ensure that they didn't fail. Their performance in previous jobs influenced my thinking process because they self-mitigated the risk of failure.

In effect, they positioned themselves well by being present and focused on success in their job, therefore being a natural choice for a promotion. They focused on meeting and exceeding expectations within their areas of responsibility, and this is something that we all can easily control. Referring back to the 100 Percent Rule, if you perform each task, no matter how small or how large, at 100 percent maximum ability, you will do well. People, sometimes important and influential people, will notice. Help make their decision to promote or reward you easy. Being the best you can be in your current position will lay the groundwork for a promotion that will continue your journey toward your best self.

Your Intention and the Process

Each morning, set your intention for the day. By doing this, your mind will focus and go into automatic search mode for things related to your intention. You'll unconsciously look for opportunities to fulfill your intention and be less likely to miss any signs of such. This is honoring the process.

You need to be keenly aware of the steps and actions required to achieve the desired result. You also need to focus your attention on each step and action to perform your best. Let's consider the example of an athlete. A football receiver is required to run their route, catch the ball and run toward the opposing goal line. If the receiver observes that the path to their objective is unobstructed, they may become excited and turn up field too quickly before catching the ball. Conversely, if they're anticipating being hit or tackled, they may also drop the ball. Analysts may comment, "He took his eye off of the ball." By not being aware and paying attention to each step necessary, they lost present focus, leaped ahead of the process, dropped the ball and forfeited an opportunity to help their team.

The true beauty of each journey is enjoying the steps along the way. If you live at 100 percent best self at all times, the eventual consequence at the end of each journey will be favorable. Decide what you want to achieve, focus on being present and doing what's necessary from moment to moment. Don't worry so much about the end result. If you focus each second on working toward your intention, it'll naturally be achieved. Let's illustrate this with another example. If you're a gardener, your intended outcome is a good crop of vegetables or beautiful flowers. Once you've set your intention, don't look too far ahead. Focus on the amount of sun required, the quality of the soil, the correct fertilizer, the amount of water needed and the threat of wildlife to your plantings. If you do this, the natural outcome will be a good harvest of vegetables and blooming flowers.

Trust the process and be patient. What you learn along the way will not only help you achieve your immediate goal but will be invaluable in the achievement of others that you're not even aware of yet. If you rush, you'll miss out on these important learnings.

I trusted the process when my family and I moved to Montreal for my career in 1999. We had difficulty adapting to our new city, and we missed being in Toronto. I found it difficult to leave my mother and friends behind. After two years, I was ready to leave. I proposed a solution whereby I would commute each week to Montreal from Toronto, but my boss didn't agree that this would work. I had no choice but to begin seeking employment in Toronto. I soon found a position in another insurance company and was ready to leave Standard Life. My boss refused to accept my letter of resignation! He asked me to wait. Within an hour, I was summoned to our president's office where he told me he was working on restructuring and would have something for me. I was to go back to Toronto, commute to Montreal, and he'd get back to me in about a month. Hmm. In one hand, I had a guaranteed offer for a VP position in Toronto, and in the other hand, I had a general verbal offer from my president. I just looked at him, shook his hand and said, "You've always been fair and treated me well. I trust you." That was that. I commuted back and forth from Toronto to Montreal, and within a few weeks, he called me and promoted me to the position of Senior Vice President, Group Insurance based in Toronto.

Gratitude

As a sales representative, I bought twenty thank you cards at the beginning of each year. They were for my underwriters in Montreal, who provided pricing quotes for me. Each time an account was sold that they'd worked on, I'd send them a card and thank them for their efforts. It was a way of thanking them for their work but it also helped to maintain focus on achieving sales target. Mailing all of the cards by the end of the year resulted in selling enough business to reach my sales objectives, and hence, my sales bonus. Every time I looked at the unsent cards on my desk, I thought of ways to drum up new business. The cards served as self-motivation and provided a Multiplier Effect to achieving my sales target. Unbeknownst to me, this initiative had an additional Multiplier Effect. One day, during my annual visit to Montreal, I noticed that my cards were pinned on the underwriters' desks. When I asked why they did this, the underwriters said they loved receiving the cards and were especially pleased when they were assigned a request for a quotation from me. They even asked their manager if they could work on my quotations specifically. They were motivated to help me sell a case so they could get a thank-you card! It was like a badge of honor for them, and it recognized their important role in the sales cycle.

Sometimes, a Multiplier Effect that is rooted in good intentions will provide additional abundance that you're not even aware of. Be present, focus 100 percent on the task at hand, and let the process work for you.

Never Be Afraid to Be Scared

Fear is good. We need to be afraid of some things. Fear helps stop us from doing harm to ourselves and others. Can you imagine if we didn't fear the consequences of our actions and words?

Fear is also a motivator that helps us focus. We study for exams for fear of failing and what that would mean. We study the real estate sales for homes in areas we are interested in for fear of overpaying and what that could mean for our monthly mortgage payments. We watch what we say carefully to loved ones for fear of upsetting them.

Fear can also be crippling if you allow it. Negative energy is draining. You don't have time to be in this state as you'll lose focus on the task at hand if your thoughts scatter in many directions.

People who are anxious about fear let it consume them, and it paralyzes their ability to live life to its fullest. When in a state of fear, simply ask yourself what you're really afraid of. What is the worst thing that could happen? How can you alleviate at least some of your fear and anxiety? More often than not, you've let your brain run wild with your negative thoughts. Things are rarely as bad as your imagination suggests.

After many years of dealing with fear, it still affects me in a negative manner, if I let it. When I first decided to pursue acting as a hobby, I auditioned for many roles, mostly non-paying. That's how you begin in the industry. You need to build your portfolio, which is a compilation of some of the roles that you've played. It's kind of like a video version of your resume. Most new actors audition for non-paying roles. These could be student films, low or no-budget short films and some low-budget indie feature films.

I recall having an audition for a student film at Toronto's arts university, the Ontario College of Art and Design (OCAD). Delighted to receive confirmation and my portion of the script, I memorized my lines and drove to OCAD. As I signed in, I glanced at the number of people who'd auditioned before me for the same role. There were at least ten names on the list. There were also three others waiting to be called in to audition from our holding area. I began to get nervous. In my corporate career, I conducted many presentations and spoke at countless charity events. Yet I was anxious in front of two film students, auditioning for a non-paying small part in a student assignment film! The fear paralyzed me, and my audition was awful. Perhaps it was fear of failure or embarrassment. I allowed my ego to drive my behavior, and my mind embellished and overestimated the negative consequences of not performing well. The fear of failure was crippling, and I didn't get the part. Upon reflection, the worst-case scenario, the one that actually transpired, was that I'd allowed myself to be embarrassed in front of two students and wouldn't get the part. Who cares? Would it have a dramatic effect on my life? Of course not. I vowed to never allow it to happen again and now memorize my lines and practice until the delivery is second nature. Trusting in myself and the process, I audition better and more confidently. If I get the role, fabulous! If not, my life is still great. Fear can be a wonderful learning tool. In this case, it was not the fear of the audition that was the learning; it was the fear of allowing my mind to exaggerate the present reality.

Fear helps keep our focus on achieving our desired results, and if we don't allow it to cripple us, it's a Multiplier Effect.

Obstacles or Opportunities?

Don't view obstacles as something negative—view them as something positive. They can be learning opportunities that help on the journey to being your best self. Each time you encounter an obstacle of some kind, there's an opportunity to focus and overcome the obstacle. This is a time to take and apply everything that you've learned, assess what's in front of you, think beyond perception and remove whatever is in your way. Sometimes, the best course of action is to just focus on performing to the best of your ability and trust the process to let events unfold as they should.

Remember one of my favorite professors, Professor Radford from Chapter 6? He once mentioned something that I often reference. He said, "Joseph, always remember that no matter how glutted the market is, there is always room for good people and good companies." He's correct, of course. Oftentimes, we think there are too many obstacles that lie in front of us, making what we seek difficult to obtain. This negative energy is destructive. But if we look further and understand the situation clearly, we may realize that opportunities exist. Be confident in your abilities as you approach each circumstance with complete self-awareness.

Is there something that's currently holding you back from being your best self? Can you look at it from a different perspective, maybe as an opportunity?

At one time, my dream job at Standard Life was to be Senior Vice-President — head of sales for all products. I had one serious obstacle in my path in the form of another VP who was also ambitious and wanted the position. They were definitely a barrier and a formidable candidate. In order to get the SVP job, I needed to clearly prove I was the natural choice. I knew that the current SVP, who would eventually retire, supported my competitor. My best course of action was to focus on my current position and exceed our goals and targets. I trusted in my abilities and my team. I also trusted the fact that good things happen to good people with good intentions. The occasional battle may be lost, but the war is usually won. I had confidence that by focusing on each step of the process, the desired end result would occur naturally. My competitor for the role was led to believe by their boss that they were the primary candidate. Did this impression make them think too far ahead and lose focus on their immediate responsibilities? I can't know, but a change was made to the corporate structure, and I was named SVP of Group Life and Health. Trust the process.

Be Patient, But Don't Wait to Ask

Always ask for what you want or for what you want to have happen in life. You can ask a person or ask the universe; it doesn't matter. Just put it out there! You'll be amazed at what will happen when you ask for something, focus on doing everything at 100 percent of your ability and be patient. As an example, if you're interested in a job opportunity that's currently unavailable, ask the manager or Human Resource department to contact you if something becomes available. Express your interest, continue to perform well within your current responsibilities and trust the process.

Meditating daily helps to clear my mind and focus on what's important to me. Sometimes, I pose a question to the universe and ask for something to happen. Then I wait. I usually receive a sign in response. Similar to setting your intention, once you've asked for something to happen, your energy automatically aligns with what's required to attain what you've asked for. Consciously and unconsciously, you'll work toward achieving what you desire, and the universe will eventually provide the opportunity to attain it. If you align your energy with the same frequency as the universe, signs of what you want will emerge.

My First "Real" Job

After I graduated from university in the mid-1980s, employment opportunities were slim. I'd worked selling shoes for the most part until then and had no intention of staying in retail. I was distraught and anxious to get my career started. My friend Mary suggested that I apply to a number of insurance companies as she had worked in the industry during the summer breaks. At first, I was reluctant because I didn't know much about the industry. She assured me that it provided many opportunities, like positions in sales, customer service, product development, IT, marketing, investments, finance and legal, to name a few. She convinced me, so I sent my CV to over twenty insurance companies. After a few weeks, Canada Life contacted me for an interview. It was the company that Mary worked for in the summer. Her aunt worked there as well, and I name-dropped her in my covering letter. Angela was my Multiplier Effect. After two sets of interviews, I was offered the position of Underwriter, US Risk. I was rich and off to the races! Coincidently, Mary joined Canada Life one month later. And yes, this is the same Mary that became my wife.

We live in an instant gratification society, constantly adjusting our focus from one thing to another too quickly. This hampers our ability to be our best selves. If we're overly concerned with wanting it all and wanting it now, we forfeit opportunities that will eventually come our way that are more beneficial for us.

The ability to focus is a powerful Multiplier Effect. If we want something to happen, we simply need to focus our attention and stay with it. If we place our full and focused attention on something specific, we naturally think, act and react in ways that are conducive to achieving what we want. This is how our minds work.

Focus, trust the process and be patient. Good things will happen.

CHAPTER 16

Be of Service

How can I best serve the universe today?

This is a question you must ask yourself each morning. How you view your role and purpose will determine how you live within your world and set the stage to become your best self. We're not just visitors here for the length of time that we live; we're woven into the fabric of our dynamic world and universe, and we each play an important role. You need to view your life as one not only well-lived for yourself but well-lived for everyone else that you share the planet with. Being of service for yourself and all things will clear the path ahead for others during your time and for future generations. Being of service means having a Multiplier Effect on yourself, others and the world.

Mentors and Sponsors

Everyone needs a mentor. Early natural mentors include our parents, grandparents, older siblings and perhaps other family members. Later on, you can select someone to be your mentor, like a professor or someone at work. Oftentimes, they naturally appear. A mentor will share information about their life experiences and provide guidance, role modeling and emotional support. You learn from mentors and they help you identify things, like career choices, that'll help you become your best.

Self-mentoring is also important. Be a trusted and experienced advisor to yourself. With complete self-awareness, who is more suited for this than yourself? A sponsor is not only someone who provides advice for development (as does a mentor) but is also someone who will advocate on your behalf. They'll actively help you advance your life. If you're fortunate enough to have a sponsor, your Multiplier Effect can be even more amplified than with a mentor. I'm grateful to have had many mentors and several sponsors in my life that have helped guide me into being the best I can be.

Eventually, we can all become mentors and sponsors. This is a natural evolution of a successful life and career and can happen at any time, but it usually happens as you gain more experience and understanding of the world. This is a great responsibility and an excellent opportunity to make a significant impact on someone. It should be taken seriously, and you should never underestimate the impact that your opinions and actions will have on the people you mentor and sponsor.

Philanthropy and Charity

Let's clarify the difference between philanthropy and charity. Philanthropy addresses the root causes of systemic issues and usually involves long-term commitments, like contributing to funding research into diseases. Charity is focused on helping in the short-term and providing immediate relief, like food and shelter to the needy.

I have always believed in giving back to the world in any way we can. This can mean volunteering your time, possessions or money, it doesn't matter. What's important is that it becomes part of who you are and what you do.

I believe that God puts us on an assembly line when he creates us. As we pass through this assembly line, different ingredients are distributed to us, good and bad. Most will get a sprinkling of kindness, a dollop of honesty, perhaps a little bit of cynicism, some meanness, and so on. Then there are some that God decides to give some extra special ingredients to—an extra helping of empathy, sympathy, caring and understanding. We must all do our best with what was handed to us to help better our world.

A simple gesture, done with the utmost sincerity, at the right time, can change someone's life.

Giving with Genuine Intentions

If you give generously with genuine intentions, the universe will reward you tenfold. Don't seek attention, acknowledgment or personal gain. Give for the sake of giving and make the world a better place because you're an active participant in it. This is one of the magical elements of humanity.

If you have the means, it's easy to donate financially to a charity or philanthropic organization. This could be an accredited and registered charity, a school fundraising event or a religious institution. Organizations need money to operate and achieve what they set out to achieve. Research hospitals need money to continue their research; buildings need to be maintained, and administrative salaries need to be paid. But volunteering your time could be more rewarding. When you volunteer, you're actively participating and can clearly see the positive effect of your actions in real time. Striking a balance between donating time and money that works for you is the ideal place to be.

I personally get more joy from volunteering. I taught mindfulness at a school to third, fourth, and fifth graders for several years, and this was the most rewarding volunteer work I've ever done. We covered deep breathing, some asanas and guided meditation. We worked on the importance of being present and breathing as a tool for anger management and stress reduction. It usually took a few classes to get buy-in from the students. At the beginning of the year there were giggles and snickers from the children, especially for the breathing exercises. However, after a few classes, they began to understand the benefits of what we were doing. As a teacher, volunteer or otherwise, there is nothing more satisfying than watching your students blossom and grow in front of your eyes.

Think of how you can help serve within your community. Serving meals at a soup kitchen, volunteering at a hospital or helping an elderly neighbor with yard work or groceries are all examples of giving time to help others. The by-product? You'll feel great!

Paving the Way for Others

Being of service includes doing things that clear the path for others to excel. There are many examples of this in history that have made a huge impact. A few that stand out for me are the abolition of slavery; women who fought for the right to vote; and the passing of the Civil Rights Act in the US in 1964 that ended segregation. These are historically significant events that were led by courageous people intent on making the lives of millions of people better. Opening such new doors for so many people not only helped them be their best selves, but just as important, paved the way for others to do the same.

My friend Tony owns a publishing and printing business in Montreal. Since 2002, he has also been printing a fabulous magazine called *Panoram Italia*. The magazine began as a passion project that is meant to help future generations understand Italian culture and its importance within Canada. I asked him why the magazine was so important to him.

"I think that it is important to remember where we came from, and although we are proud Canadians, our Italian heritage, language, culture and traditions still form a part of who we are and who our children and grandchildren will be." I admire Tony for being of service to the Italian community.

Jackie Robinson, a professional baseball player, became the first African American player to play in the major leagues in the modern era. He understood what this meant to his personal safety and was prepared to make the sacrifice for the benefit of all future African American baseball players. This ushered in a new era of opportunity for more players.

Bertha Wilson was the first woman appointed to the Supreme Court of Canada in 1982. By 2020, four out of nine judges on the Supreme Court of Canada were women. Ms. Wilson helped lay the foundation of a more gender-balanced makeup of the Supreme Court. Being a trailblazer who lessens the obstacles for others who follow in your footsteps or helps others achieve their best selves is being of service.

> *Someone can make you feel much more special in a short period of time than someone else in a much longer period of time.*

Not all things need to be done on such a large scale to be impactful. Everything has an impact. I learned more from the young students to whom I taught mindfulness than they did from me. Before each class, I'd ask them what random acts of kindness they'd done since we last met. The responses were remarkable. They mentioned sharing their lunch with someone who forgot theirs, standing up for a friend who was being bullied or just saying thank you to their bus driver. These are all small acts of being of service that have an extraordinary impact.

Sharing

Sharing is one of the most important things that you can do to be of service. Oxford's Lexico site defines sharing as giving a portion of something to someone or using or occupying a space with others. These definitions of sharing are perfectly acceptable, but what do they mean to you?

Now let's define sharing much more broadly through a global lens—there are things that all of us share with each other always. In this context, *what is mine is yours, and what is yours is mine.* Nothing that is mine, is mine in its entirety. It's also yours and everyone else's. This includes the oceans, the stars and the air that we breathe. Space and time are also shared with everyone. At a high level, the planet that we live on is shared with billions of other human beings and other forms of life. We need to respect this and maintain the delicate balance that is nature. We cannot assume, just because we consider ourselves the species of the highest intelligence, that we can do what we want to the planet and environment without considering its effect on other forms of life. We need to consider the impact of our actions on everyone and everything. We are one with all things and everything that everyone does is linked together in some form. Sharing of this nature carries a great responsibility because it has implications not just for today, but for generations to come.

On the other hand, there is the concept of what is mine is yours and vice-versa; sharing with the people you love and have the closest emotional and physical ties. We share possessions and emotions with the people we are closest to. Families, as an example, share living arrangements and the responsibilities of running a household. In my family, not much is solely anyone's as we share most things in one manner or another. We need to understand and respect this dynamic. Our most beloved share is of our dogs Frankie and Leo!

On yet another scale, you might experience situational sharing for a period. At work, it could be sharing office space, car-pooling or the cafeteria. At school, it could be sharing your notes with a classmate who was absent from class. It is limited to a specific amount of time, but important to helping you be your best self during this period. As mentioned in an earlier chapter, I co-produced and participated as an actor in an independent film. It was an incredible learning experience. Being a low-budget project, we shared dressing rooms, holding areas, costumes, makeup and bathrooms. If we needed something, we determined how to handle the need together. If we needed a car, actors and crew provided theirs, and if we required luggage for a scene, people brought theirs from home. If our makeup artist required a portable steamer, someone brought theirs. Two actors even offered their homes as locations for several scenes. Everyone selflessly volunteered their time and possessions completely with the single purpose of trying to make the film as successful as it could be. This is situational sharing at its best. I have been lucky enough to meet many genuine and kind people in my life. Antonio Musano is one of these. Antonio and I worked together for many years at Standard Life. Antonio was my go-to IT person and a significant Multiplier Effect. Whenever I experienced an issue with technology, be it my BlackBerry or laptop, Antonio always quickly solved the problem. Antonio and a group of friends raise money each year through a variety of events to help children's hospitals. Antonio expressed his feelings perfectly: "I have been very blessed to have a great family and good friends in my life. Helping sick children and children from less fortunate families is near and dear to my heart. I just feel good when I help." His enthusiasm and energy directed toward this cause continue to grow each year. It's clear that Antonio's passion for helping children has helped him toward becoming the best that he can be. This applies to all who give back to their communities. Their work is a Multiplier Effect and the results of their efforts supports the recipients in their journey toward being their best selves.

Giving back to the community in which you live and work helps you become who you are, and it just feels good. Feeling good elevates your mood and makes you happy, and when you're happy, you're more prone to do things that make you better.

At all times, we are sharing something with each other, with nature and the world. Understanding this connection and coexisting in harmony with the world is being of service to it.

Be generous, kind, thoughtful and respectful of all living things, and most of all, be grateful for what the world offers all of us. Being alive and being of service is a privilege.

CHAPTER 17

Mental and Physical Fitness

The obvious benefits of being physically fit include lowered blood pressure, cholesterol management, bone loss prevention, as well as circulation, respiration and digestion health. The benefits of good mental condition are many and well documented, and you can't be at your best if you're not mentally and physically fit. The two are linked as physical activity can lower instances of depression, anxiety, emotional pain and loneliness.

In one way or another, I've always maintained a certain level of physical activity throughout my life. I always tried to maintain a fitness schedule in my corporate life even if sometimes life and work got in the way. I could spend an extraordinary amount of time sitting at my desk, literally hours looking at my desktop screen or reading reports. When I realized that this was happening, I'd catch myself and walk up and down the twenty flights of stairs in our building. The time it took out of my busy day was worth it because my energy levels increased substantially. I'm convinced that having some form of a physical fitness routine, no matter how sporadic, helped me manage my hectic schedule throughout my career.

The Marathon Man

As mentioned earlier, my first corporate job was as an underwriter of US health risk for a company called Canada Life. It was 1986, and I'd just left York University. I was young, energetic, ambitious, and worked in a department filled with similar personalities. I loved my time at Canada Life. It was very progressive in its belief that good physical health affects productivity in the workplace. It even sponsored a study with the University of Toronto regarding the effects of physical activity and absenteeism in the workplace. The results were encouraging, and Canada Life, to my knowledge, was the first company in the insurance sector to build an in-house fitness facility. This included aerobic classes, gym equipment and various sponsored corporate teams—basketball, volleyball, baseball and running. I was on the volleyball and running teams. I even taught aerobics classes. Canada Life embraced flex-time schedules and encouraged all of its employees to use the facilities as long as workloads were managed.

Canada Life had many runners, and I contemplated attempting to run the 1987 Toronto Wang Marathon. A vice president within our division, an avid and experienced runner himself, advised against it because I was relatively new to the sport and had never run anywhere near the length of a marathon. I didn't have enough "garbage miles" accumulated, according to him. Garbage miles are miles accumulated by running for long periods of time. This lets your body get used to the strain and effort of long distances. Using an article in *Runner's World* magazine that gave advice on how to train for your first marathon, I accepted the challenge and was off to the (literal) races!

Unfortunately, during this period, my dad was diagnosed with lung cancer. He underwent surgery to remove a large tumor, but it was too late. We soon found out that cancer had spread to his brain. The location of the tumor meant that surgery was not an option, and radiation treatment began. My family knew that he was terminal, but no one talked about it. He was only sixty years old, and I was twenty-six. I trained for the marathon during my lunch breaks at Canada Life during the week and ran on Saturday mornings. The routes ran through downtown Toronto and along Lake Ontario. I trained alone, and some of the runs lasted well over an hour. During this time, it seemed as if my body went into a moving meditative state. I thought about my dad, what he required in terms of treatment on any given day, what appointments to make and how to relieve my mom of her burden of caring for him.

Sometimes, I'd spend the entire time during training runs talking to my dad. I'd get angry at him for not quitting smoking and would apologize for not spending enough time with him. Other times, I'd talk to God, and when especially angry or just wanting to understand, I'd try to arrange a three-way conversation between God, my dad and me. Questions were asked and satisfactory answers never received. These solo therapy sessions helped me, and I never felt alone. Training for the marathon served as moving meditation and helped me deal with the mental anguish and stress of watching my father fade away to a shadow of himself during his eight months living with cancer.

Sometimes you just need to draw the shades, turn off the lights and call it a day. And meditate.

Meditation and Pranayama to the Rescue

Everyone can benefit from meditating. Take the time to quiet your mind and be grateful for all of the abundance that's available to you. There is always something specific that we can be appreciative of, like health, family and friends. I prefer quiet meditation each morning, alternating between meditating while lying in bed and in a seated position, usually before sunrise. It helps clear my mind and prepare for the day ahead. On occasion, meditating in the evening, quite often before falling asleep in bed, helps me reflect upon the day. This usually occurs when the day didn't turn out quite as expected. I practice being in the moment and not letting the past affect my present, but sometimes, I stumble. Meditation helps calm my senses and reminds me of what's most important to me in my life. It helps bring everything back into proper perspective and allows me to have a good night's rest.

The various types of meditation that are covered in Chapter 4 will give you the information needed to decide which type works for you.

Pranayama breathing, the yogic practice of breath regulation, is also very important in maintaining good mental and physical health. It helps to calm the mind. There are several methods and each have their own specific benefits. Two techniques that I use often is alternate nostril breathing or simply taking slow, deep inhales and exhales. My personal preferred types of pranayama breathing are described in greater detail in Appendix II.

Mr. Clean

Good grooming habits, overall cleanliness and personal hygiene contribute to good mental and physical health. The physical health benefits are obvious. Clean hands, nails, hair and body help to suppress the spread of germs and illness. This has recently been especially evident during the Covid-19 global pandemic. One of the earliest and most effective strategies to control the spread of the illness, in addition to wearing face masks, was to wash your hands regularly with soap and use hand sanitizer. It took a pandemic to remind us just how important handwashing is.

Clean clothing also helps prevent the spread of germs and impurities. This is important if you have been ill or have been exposed to someone who is sick. Washing clothing on a regular basis, mostly after each use, helps to ensure that your garments are germ-free and smell fresh.

The social benefits of good hygiene are also to be considered. Bathing regularly and wearing clean clothing reduce the possibility of body odor and the negative stigma and embarrassment attached to it.

Admit it, don't you feel good after showering? How about wearing your just-washed favorite sweater or climbing into bed to the smell of fresh bedsheets? Yes, I thought so.

Dress for Mental Health

I'm a firm believer that when you look good, you feel good. In addition to good grooming and personal hygiene habits, dressing well and appropriately for the occasion can contribute to positive mental health and productivity. I've retired from a full-time corporate life, but I still wake up early in the morning, read my papers, confirm the day's agenda, shower and dress according to the day's activities.

Dressing appropriately is one of my Multiplier Effects. If I'm scheduled to attend a board meeting, even if it's held remotely through videoconference, dressing as if attending in person helps me be at my best. A suit and tie may not always be necessary, but a shirt and jacket usually work well. Doing this helps me mentally prepare for the meeting.

Can you think of ways that your attire can serve as a Multiplier Effect for being your best? As an example, when reading a book or gathering information on a topic of interest, do you dress in very casual and comfortable clothing, just as you did to study for exams during school? Perhaps you have specific gardening shoes, workout runners or a comfortable blanket just for watching television? Do you have an article of clothing or an accessory of some sort that just makes you feel good when you wear it? A lucky shirt, perhaps? All of these, and your other personal favorites serve as Multiplier Effects for helping you be the best that you can be.

Music for Mental Health

Music has been a part of my life for as long as I can remember, and I listen to it almost all day, every day, no matter what I'm doing.

Science has confirmed that there is a clear link between music and mood. Listening to music that you enjoy elevates your mood and can even release melatonin and norepinephrine, both mood-elevating substances in our brains. Have you ever witnessed an enthusiastic karaoke singer? How about someone singing up a storm while driving? That's what I'm talking about.

Music preference is a personal choice, and I select my playlist based on my mood or the mood that I want to be in, not necessarily the mood that I'm actually in. My mood and attitude can change simply by playing the music of a specific genre that speaks to me at that moment. Experiment listening to music from all genres, cultures and eras. Finding something that works for you can have a very powerful Multiplier Effect on your ability to perform tasks because it helps place you in a state of mind that is conducive to having success in any particular moment.

Get your Z's

Imagine if there was one single thing that could thwart your ability to be your best self in everything that you do. What would that be for you? If you imagined sleep, you'd be absolutely correct. Quantity and quality of sleep is important in maintaining good physical and mental health. Sleep and overall health are interconnected as poor sleep habits can lead to poor health and poor health leads to poor sleep habits. Each of us is unique in the amount of sleep we require each night and knowing what works best for you is important.

A good night's rest has a powerful Multiplier Effect on your ability to perform at 100 percent at all times. If you're sleep deprived, you' simply won't be physically and mentally prepared for the day's activities. Think of an activity that you undertake each day. Examples could be driving, preparing a meal, attending a yoga class, helping children with homework or simply having a conversation with a friend. If you're physically and mentally tired because of a lack of sleep, how would you handle the activity? Now, think of how you'd perform the same activity with a good night's rest. There would be quite a difference, wouldn't you agree?

Holistic and Traditional Medicine Healing

It is important that we look at all possible forms of treatment that can help us if we are not feeling well. Can cures and treatments with traditional medicine work together with a holistic approach? Absolutely! I view them as complementary, not independent of each other. Anyone who favors one approach over the other is sacrificing the Multiplier Effect that each approach offers. Holistic treatments can often treat conditions on their own or enhance the effectiveness of traditional medicine.

Integrative medicine, which is a holistic medical discipline that considers the mind, body and soul of a patient during the treatment process, can be beneficial for certain ailments when combined with a more traditional approach, including drug therapy. As holistic medicine is becoming better understood for its practical application and success, such practices are becoming more and more common.

Reiki, a form of alternative medicine called energy healing, is a holistic multiplier on its own. Universal energy is transferred through the palms of a practitioner to encourage physical and emotional healing. I am a Reiki Master and have seen firsthand the powerful effects that Reiki can have. I've treated many students, family, even pets, and the results have been very positive. Often, especially for physical ailments, Reiki treatments are combined with drug therapy and rehabilitative exercise.

The Treatment Ladder

In my opinion, there is a sequence for the prevention and cure of illness and disease. The first step, of course, is proper self-care. This includes eating well, staying hydrated, engaging in a regular exercise routine and meditation. This will help to prevent illness.

If an illness presents itself, the first curative approach should be holistic in nature. Depending on the ailment, different eating habits, herbal medicines, reflexology, aromatherapy, body massage, acupuncture, Reiki and a host of other options are available. Lifestyle, attitude, spiritual health as well as mental health are to be considered. The idea is to treat the person first. Sometimes, if underlying conditions are treated, the ailment is alleviated. A good example is all of the negative issues that are related to stress. Instead of treating stress related high blood pressure with medicine, a holistic approach will look at the underlying causes of the stress. If this is dealt with, the stress will be alleviated and blood pressure will return to normal levels. A holistic approach is especially effective for chronic conditions.

The next step, if necessary, is traditional medicine, including drug therapy, and in more extreme cases, surgery. Too often in Western society, we're quick to turn to traditional medicine as the first step to curing something. If we have a headache, many will immediately reach for a tablet in search of relief. This temporary solution can work if the issue is isolated but is not healthy as a long-term solution. If I have a headache, the first thing that I do is consider how much water I've consumed during the day. Dehydration commonly results in headaches, and I've taken care of many headaches simply by drinking a couple of glasses of water.

This is a stepladder approach that will ensure that you're considering all treatments available to take care of what ails you and enhance your ability to be your best self.

The Yoga Asanas

Initially, I, like many in Western society, believed yoga was strictly a physical discipline in the form of asanas or physical postures. I didn't care for yoga, nor did I have any interest in learning much about it.

One day, my family suggested giving a yoga class a try. Suffering from back problems, most likely as a result of countless hours spent on airplanes, in offices and in boardrooms, I thought, "Why not?" It was a hot vinyasa yoga class, and I was immediately taken by its intensity and how physically exhausted I was after practice. I was quickly hooked.

There are many types of yoga, and with a bit of experimenting, you'll find which style works best for you. Hatha and vinyasa yoga are favorites of mine. The strength, flexibility and breathing control associated with these forms of yoga asanas are best suited for me.

Today, I'm a certified yoga instructor who teaches and practices on a regular basis and I'm convinced that a consistent yoga practice, combined with meditation and pranayama breathing, is the fountain of youth. I've experienced firsthand its benefits and have helped many students on their personal path to becoming their best self.

So what are you doing to be physically and mentally fit? Write down your answers below.

_____

_____

_____

_____

_____

_____

Now, if you could add just one thing to the list, what would it be?

Select a physical activity that works for you and incorporate it into your regular routine. Pranayama breathing, walking, running, hiking, yoga asanas, gardening or organized sports all work well. Consistency is key.

Physical and mental fitness are very important Multiplier Effects that help you gain the physical strength and stamina required to perform at a peak level during difficult times. They help quiet and clear the mind so you can focus on what's important.

CONCLUSION

If you were to be asked, "What is your most important Multiplier Effect?" how would you respond? Write it down here:

_____

Let's read a poem that my friend Kym and I wrote, which will explain my thinking on what this is.

You Are She

She was deep. A primal soul with universal energy
as illuminating as the night sky
One man's darkness is another man's light,
and she was light and darkness for all
Conceived within, nourished by the good of mankind,
dimmed by its madness

Yet she stood still, on the edges of that insanity,
just to shine for them and light their way home
Grounded in the faith of humanity
and with the stoic defiance of all obstacles,
she looked up toward the ultimate of jewels . . .
the Crown

Not all understood that the journey began
when they reached home
So after many long and tangled miles
of safely guiding many lost souls
She led the understanding man to his gate of destiny

Smiling with a quiet confidence
and reassuring voice,
she leaned over and whispered . . . rise
Rise to heights unimaginable.
Rise from the depths of the Pacific
to the heights of Bellatrix.
Rise to hear the explosion within,
for you are reborn to create a new world

And as she whispered, the path ahead lit
like a summer sunrise, and he knew
Here he would grow only flowers
With eyes closed and eyes open
he knew what needed to be done and undone . . .
the first new step is taken

If your answer was self-awareness, excellent!

I have asked you to respond to many questions throughout this book. Now I'll ask you several more, and just to make it easy for you, I'll also provide the answers.

1. Am I capable of unleashing my best self? YES!
2. Do I have a special purpose in the universe? YES!
3. Is happiness a choice, and do I choose to be happy? YES!
4. Am I constantly striving to be joyful? YES!
5. Am I doing the best that I can every minute of every day? YES!
6. Do I have an abundance of talent? YES!
7. Do I wake up every day grateful for what I have? YES!

8. Is the world a better place because of me? YES!
9. Do I love myself? YES!
10. Am I always looking for Multiplier Effects in my life? YES!

Life is amazing, and your journey is a never-ending series of wonderful experiences. We are all flawed, yet beautifully so. View life as a never-ending journey of learning and discovery. We are in debt to the abundance of the universe and are obligated to share everything we have to offer with it. Discover all the Multiplier Effects that will help you to be the best that you can be. They are everywhere and easily available. Simply pause and reflect on what they might be in each circumstance, and your story will unfold as it's meant to.

The universe needs you and the constantly evolving you is perfect in the moment. Remember when I asked you what your story was at the beginning of the book? Has it changed? What will be your story now?

For all of us, unfinished is the perfect state to be in.

APPENDIX I

Living Above the Heart Chakra

Most of us have heard of Chakras, or at least the seven main ones. The foundational one, the Root Chakra, is located at the base of our spine and the rest move along upwards until we reach the Crown Chakra, located at the top of our heads. There are actually 114 of them in our bodies (although some believe that there are 112). They serve as points of energy that flow throughout the body. For well-being, energy needs to flow freely through the main Chakras. If one of the Chakras is "blocked" in any way, this energy flow is disrupted, and your ability to be at your 100 percent best is hampered. Think of this energy flow as a long hallway with seven doors that leads you to your ideal destination at the end. If all of the doors are open, your path is clear and smooth. However, if one or more of the doors is closed, your journey will be interrupted until you find a way to open them. Therefore, caring for your main Chakras is very important and will have a Multiplier Effect for you. There are many excellent reference sources to learn about your Chakras. I have briefly summarized the seven main Chakras for you below so you have an idea of what they are and what they represent.

Crown Chakra: This energy point is located at the very top of the head. It represents a state of bliss and being in and having a connection with a higher state of being. This could be a connection to universal energy or God.

Third Eye Chakra: This Chakra is located at a spot on the lower forehead in between the eyebrows about an inch or so above the bridge of the nose. This is an important Chakra because it represents intuition, wisdom and knowledge. It is an internal eye that helps "see" things that are not visible with our eyes. Opening the third eye will require some work with your pineal gland, but trust me, when it is opened, you will see and understand things much differently.

Throat Chakra: As the name implies, this Chakra is located at the throat. It represents speaking the truth about ourselves and everything around us. It means having complete and honest self-awareness.

Heart Chakra: Where else would this be located but in the heart area? It represents everything we think of when we think of the heart at an emotional level—unconditional love and compassion.

Solar Plexus Chakra: This Chakra is located at the core of the body below the chest. Think of strong willpower, "internal fortitude" or "internal fire," and you will understand the meaning and importance of this Chakra.

Sacral Chakra: This Chakra is located below the navel and above the sexual organs. It reflects sexuality and a sense of pleasure. Interestingly, it also represents creativity and emotions.

Root Chakra: This Chakra is one of the most important Chakras in my opinion. Located at the base of the spine, it represents our basic foundation for growth as human beings—grounding, the stability of having all of the basic needs for survival, including food, water and shelter. Think of this Chakra as the foundation of a house. If the foundation is not strong, no matter what materials were used to build it, it will not be stable.

The Heart Chakra, located at the center of all of the Chakras, divides the top three from the bottom three. I often speak of living above and below the Heart Chakra and how important it is to understand the difference between the two.

Living below the Heart Chakra means living in survival mode—for the most part focusing solely on food, shelter and reproduction. Think of the major physical functions that happen below our hearts. This is where we take care of the basic needs necessary to exist. Some of us prefer to live here. It's safe and simple. I respect anyone's decision to do so but don't understand it. The reason I say this is because there is so much more to aspire to. If you truly want to make a difference in your life and in the lives of others and leave the world a better place, you'll need to go beyond mere survival and begin to live above the Heart Chakra.

Living spiritually is living above the Heart Chakra. This means living in a world that transcends the physical and moves into the spiritual. If you do this, the physical part of being is less emphasized and will work in harmony with the spiritual part. The physical nature of beings begins to take on less importance. You'll begin to place greater emphasis on what is in the hearts, minds and souls of humans. If you care less about the physical nature of people, you'll care less about what they look like. Such things as size, color, race, sexual orientation and religious affiliation will play a lesser role, or ideally, a nonexistent role, in determining your attitude and the nature of your relationship with each person. The physical aspects will simply not take on as much importance. This allows you to eliminate perceived boundaries that limit your ability to draw on the entire populace for help in achieving your best self. You'll appreciate others as spiritual and energy beings more than as physical beings. This implies much more greatness—you'll be more inclined to draw and attract from a greater base of humanity to help you through your journey to greatness.

Living above the Heart Chakra also helps you to know, understand and respect your place in the world and universe. It opens you up to the infinite possibilities available to you as you explore your relationship with others and with all things.

One of the key understandings in my personal experience as I've awakened is my relationship with all living beings. I'm clear in comprehending that humans are the species of the highest intellect and evolution on our planet. I'm also very clear on the premise that just because this is so, I don't have a greater right to the planet than other living beings. All living things share the planet. I now, to the best of my ability, live in harmony and coexistence with all living things. This includes plants, trees, animals, insects, fish and, of course, other human beings.

Do your best to live and exemplify good values and always have a high moral standard. Lead by example and make certain that your words match your actions. I falter on occasion, certainly, but I'm fine with that because all I can do is be the best that I can be with the time that I have.

One of my mentors, Jocelyn Proteau, who was chair of our Canadian board of directors once shared great words of wisdom, "Joseph, do the right thing, always. It won't be easy, and sometimes the pressure to do something against your values will be intense. Do not compromise. Maintain your integrity. You will want to be remembered as leaving not through the side or back door of life, but through the front door, with your head held high." Jocelyn is a very wise man.

Be kind and respectful of all living things and strive to live above the Heart Chakra. Our energy is universal, and we can all be Multiplier Effects for each other.

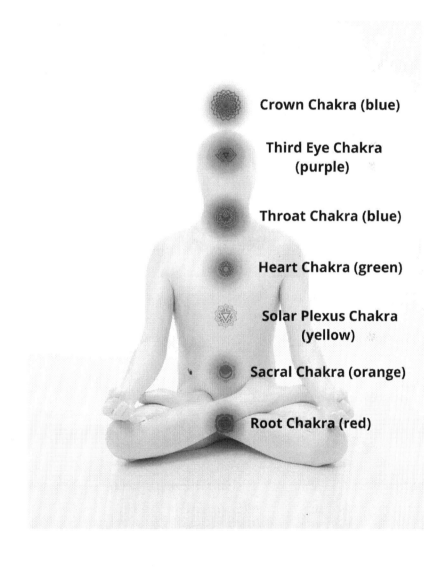

Crown Chakra (blue)

Third Eye Chakra (purple)

Throat Chakra (blue)

Heart Chakra (green)

Solar Plexus Chakra (yellow)

Sacral Chakra (orange)

Root Chakra (red)

APPENDIX II

My Three Favorite Types of Pranayama Breathing

1. Alternate Nostril Breathing (Nadi Shodhana)

This breathing technique is effective to clear and calm the mind, especially for stress relief.

- Sit in a comfortable seated position, preferably cross-legged.
- Use your dominant hand (because I am right-handed, the example will reflect this).
- Exhale completely and use your right thumb to close your right nostril.
- Inhale deeply with your left nostril. Close your left nostril with your right ring finger. Hold for a few seconds. I usually count to 8 or even 16.
- Release and exhale completely through the right nostril.
- Inhale deeply through the right nostril, then close. Hold for the same amount of time as your opposite nostril.
- Open the left nostril and exhale completely.

I perform 5–10 cycles.

2. Ocean Breath (Ujjayi Pranayama)

I perform Ujjayi breathing throughout my yoga practices as well as when relaxing reading a book or listening to music. Sometimes I take a few breaths before falling asleep. I even use this breathing technique if I begin to feel anxious, angry or frustrated. It helps calm me down.

If you have ever taken a yoga class, your teacher has more than likely encouraged you to "focus on your ujjayi breath."

- Begin in any comfortable position, standing, sitting or lying down.
- Take a deep breath through your nose or mouth.
- Exhale through your nose while constricting the back of your throat. The most common metaphor I use is to imagine trying to fog up a mirror with your exhale.
- Continue to breathe deeply in this manner for 3 to 5 minutes, constricting the back of your throat. Notice how you feel.

3. Fire Breathing (Kapalabhati Pranayama)

As its name implies, this technique will create internal heat and help warm you up. As this can be an intense breathing exercise for beginners, begin by doing 10 or 20 cycles and build up to as many as you feel comfortable doing. I usually do this breathing for 3 to 5 minutes at a time. The obvious physical benefits are strengthening of the stomach muscles and diaphragm, but I just feel better overall when I'm done.

- Begin in a comfortable seated cross-legged position, resting your hands on your knees.

- Inhale deeply through your nose.
- Exhale forcefully, contracting your core muscles.
- Once you exhale forcefully, you will find that you naturally inhale, so there is no need to purposefully inhale.
- Keep repeating.

ABOUT THE AUTHOR

Joseph Iannicelli was raised in a traditional home of Italian immigrants who taught him that hard work was the pathway to success. Joseph has spent his entire professional career in the financial services industry, including serving as President and CEO of Standard Life Assurance Company of Canada. Joseph currently serves on boards and is a life coach. Additionally, he is a yoga teacher and Reiki master, and you'll even see him as the lead actor in the indie film *Crimson Sands*. He realizes that full self-awareness and maximizing one's potential, personally and professionally, brings happiness and joyfulness. He considers himself on an endless journey towards becoming his best self, while enjoying everything life has to offer. He's always looking forward to what's next, knowing that whatever it is, it'll be fun!

Everything comes to an end,
but the end is never-ending.

Manufactured by Amazon.ca
Bolton, ON

35267324R00134